Why Won't My Children Talk to Me? A Book For Conservatives

Bradley Hall

Published by Bradley Hall, 2023.

WHY WON'T MY CHILDREN TALK TO ME? A BOOK FOR CONSERVATIVES

First edition. September 6, 2023.

Copyright © 2023 Bradley Hall.

ISBN: 979-8223228790

Written by Bradley Hall.

Table of Contents

This book is dedicated to all of those, liberals and conservatives, who are trying to establish or maintain a relationship with their parents and children, no matter where they may fall on the political landscape.

Introduction

"The greatest mistake of any movement is to go against human nature. We may be conservative by nature, but that doesn't mean we have to be impossible to tolerate."

These poignant words have resonated with me deeply as I embarked on the journey of writing this book. As an American with a passion for this country, I have come face to face with one of the most pressing issues plaguing our society today – the growing divide between conservatives and their adult children.

In the vast tapestry of family dynamics, there exists a troubling rift, an unbridgeable chasm that separates parents from their own flesh and blood. Why won't my children talk to me? A question that reverberates through the minds of countless conservatives who find themselves at odds with the very ones they raised, nurtured, and loved. In this book, aptly titled "Why Won't My Children Talk to Me? A Book For Conservatives." I aim to delve deep into the heart of this problem, seeking not just answers, but also a path to healing and reconciliation.

This book is not an attack on conservatives; it is a call to introspection, a plea for self-examination. In a world where individualism and personal freedom are prized above all else, the clash between conservative values and the evolving perspectives of the younger generation has reached a boiling point. It is time to confront the reality that perhaps the problem lies not with the children, but with the very foundations upon which conservatism is built.

For example, just a few weeks ago, my father and I engaged in an intense discussion. I had half-jokingly commented that I would vote for Jimmy Carter if he ran in the next election and my father retorted, "Do you know what you get if you vote for Carter? You get a 55-MPH speed limit!" Despite me showing him many sources showing it was Richard Nixon who did this, he doubled down and said, "Well, I'll still believe it was Carter!"

This is just one anecdotal incident I have encountered. When presented with evidence from any source, they double down, claim it to be "Fake News" or "Leftist Propaganda" and double down on whatever they believed to begin with.

Conservatives believe Gen X, Gen Y, and Gen Z to all be children, despite many of us being in our 30s and 40s. They call all of us "Millennials" and laugh at "Participation Trophies" when their generation was the one that created them. Their disdain for our generations is due to the fact that, while they made us, they failed at making us in their image. "You'll become more conservative as you get older!" is a common refrain, but the opposite has been true for so many of us.

Throughout these pages, I will unveil the layers of this intricate issue, peeling back the misconceptions and challenging the deeply ingrained beliefs that have driven this divide. It is not enough to ponder the question, 'Why won't my children talk to me?' We must also confront the painful truth that your own rigid ideologies may be the root cause.

WHY WON'T MY CHILDREN TALK TO ME? A BOOK FOR CONSERVATIVES

My goal is not to belittle, condemn, or alienate conservatives, but to ignite a spark of self-awareness. For too long, the voices of the frustrated children have been dismissed, their desires for open dialogue and mutual respect cast aside in favor of political agendas and entrenched beliefs. The time has come for conservatives to step outside their comfort zones and truly listen, to seek understanding rather than conformity.

In these pages, I will challenge long-held assumptions, debunk myths, and offer a fresh perspective on conservatism in the context of modern society. Drawing from extensive research, personal experiences, and thought-provoking interviews, I will shine a light on the pain points and complications that have caused this breakdown in communication.

We cannot find solutions without first acknowledging the problem. I will guide you through a journey that is equal parts introspective and immersive. We will explore the delicate balance between tradition and progress, personal values and societal change, while uncovering the underlying reasons why your children may have distanced themselves.

This is not a call to conversion; it is an invitation to empathy. By understanding the perspectives of both conservatives and their children, we can begin to bridge the gap and foster a new era of understanding and respect. It is not an easy path, but it is a necessary one.

So, my dear readers, I implore you to embark on this journey with an open heart and an open mind. Let us confront the painful truth and seek a way forward. Together, we can mend the broken bonds, rebuild the lines of communication, and create a future where conservative parents and their children can coexist harmoniously.

Join me, as we challenge the status quo, confront our own biases, and strive to make amends. Let us embark on this transformative quest – not just for the sake of our own families, but for the future of conservatism itself.

The answers we seek lie not in the broad strokes of political rhetoric, but in the intimate stories of our own lives. We will uncover the truth, one page at a time.

Are you ready to delve into the heart of this complex issue? Are you willing to take that first step towards understanding, healing, and reconciliation? If so, turn the page, for the journey awaits.

Chapter 1: Understanding the Generation Gap

The Changing Landscape of Values

In the ever-evolving tapestry of society, the values that once anchored us seem to shift like grains of sand beneath our feet. It is within this changing landscape of values that we find ourselves grappling with a disheartening reality – our children, our own flesh and blood, have chosen to distance themselves from us. As conservatives, we must not shy away from the introspection required to understand why. We must confront the genuine possibility that our own rigid ideologies may be the root cause.

We live in an era where media and technology have become intertwined with our daily lives, shaping our thoughts, beliefs, and perspectives. The constant access to digital platforms has exposed individuals to diverse narratives, ideas, and values. Our children, raised in this digital age, have been immersed in a world far different from the one you knew. They have encountered perspectives and viewpoints that challenge the very foundations of conservative beliefs, leading to clashes within our families.

The march of time leaves its indelible mark on each generation, etching their values deep into their core. While you, as conservatives, hold steadfast to traditions rooted in our own experiences, our children have been shaped by different historical events, cultural shifts, and experiences. The generational divide that often exists between conservative parents and their non-conservative children gives rise to a clash of values, creating tension and estrangement within our families.

The clash between traditional conservative values and progressive values is akin to colliding tectonic plates, threatening to fracture the familial bonds we hold dear. As society has embraced progress in areas such as LGBTQ+ rights, racial equality, and climate change, we find ourselves at odds with our children and their generation. These disharmonious values can be like a canyon, separating us and causing pain and resentment on both sides.

The changing roles and expectations within families add yet another layer of complexity to the landscape of values. Traditional gender roles have evolved, and expectations regarding gender equality, work-life balance, and parenting styles have shifted. These changes can create disconnects between conservative parents who may still adhere to traditional gender roles and their non-conservative children, who champion equal opportunities and freedom of choice.

Economic factors can exert a powerful influence on our values and create divisions within families. Differing financial circumstances, job insecurity, or conflicting views on wealth distribution can exacerbate tensions between conservative parents and their non-conservative children. These economic disparities can manifest as clashes over individual responsibility, social safety nets, and the redistribution of resources, further widening the separation between us.

In an interconnected world where cultural exchange is increasingly prevalent, globalization has ushered in cultural value shifts. Exposure to different perspectives, beliefs, and cultural norms has influenced societal values, often clashing with the traditional conservatism many of us hold dear. These conflicting values can strain relationships within our families, as we struggle to reconcile our deeply ingrained beliefs with those of our children.

Education, a cornerstone of personal growth and intellectual development, can also become a point of contention within families. Higher education, critical thinking, and exposure to diverse ideas often foster progressive values in our children. However, these values may directly conflict with the conservative ideals you have instilled in them. The divergent intellectual values between parents and children can lead to strained communication and emotional turmoil.

Religion, an anchor of moral and ethical beliefs, can both unite and divide families. Conservative parents and their non-conservative children may have differing religious beliefs or interpretations, leading to conflicts over moral values. As the landscape of religious practice evolves alongside societal changes, our children's departure from conservative religious beliefs can serve as a source of deep anguish and misunderstanding. Indoctrination is usually a word bandied about regarding the religious beliefs of others, but, when a child is instituted into the religion of their parents, is this not also a form of indoctrination?

In the face of these value conflicts, it is paramount that you understand the importance of open dialogue and respect. The key to bridging the gap lies in fostering healthy communication, seeking understanding, and finding common ground within our families. By embracing open-mindedness and empathy, you can create an environment that allows for genuine connection and unity, even in the face of differing values.

Value conflicts have the potential to strain family relationships to their breaking point. Emotional turmoil, strained communication, and broken bonds permeate these conflicts, tearing at the fabric of our most cherished connections. The pain of feeling alienated from our own children is a heavy burden to bear, and the toll it takes on both parents and children cannot be overstated.

Yet, even in the face of such crushing difficulties, there is hope for redemption and renewed family bonds. Navigating value conflicts requires a willingness to compromise, display empathy, and find shared values that can bridge the deep chasms between us. By embracing the challenges and facing them head-on with love, understanding, and a commitment to growth, you can forge stronger family bonds and begin to heal the wounds inflicted by differing values.

In moments of despair, when the divide feels insurmountable, seeking professional support can provide a lifeline. Family therapy or counseling can create a safe space for open dialogue and facilitate understanding between parents and children. In the hands of a neutral third party, communication can be nurtured, wounds can be healed, and the path to reconciliation can be paved.

The changing landscape of values presents a formidable challenge to conservative parents seeking to reconcile with their non-conservative children. By embarking on a journey of understanding, empathy, and self-reflection, we can confront your own biases and create a future where conservative values are not just acknowledged but also respected and understood. Together, let us embark on this transformative quest, for the sake of our children, ourselves, and the future of conservatism.

Communicating Across Generations

ONE OF THE PRIMARY obstacles in communication between conservative parents and non-conservative children lies in their different communication styles and preferences. Conservative parents may prefer direct, authoritative communication, while non-conservative children tend to value open-ended discussions and collaborative decision-making.

These differences can often lead to misunderstandings and conflicts, as each party may feel unheard or invalidated. For effective communication to take place, both parties must acknowledge and adapt to each other's communication styles, finding common ground that respects both authority and individual autonomy.

Active listening serves as the foundation for effective communication. It requires fully engaging with the speaker and making a genuine effort to understand their perspective. Conservative parents can enhance their active listening skills by maintaining eye contact, asking clarifying questions, and avoiding interruptions. By actively listening, conservative parents show their non-conservative children that they value their thoughts and opinions, creating a safe space for meaningful dialogue.

Empathy plays a vital role in bridging the gap between conservative parents and non-conservative children. It involves putting oneself in the other person's shoes and truly understanding their emotions and experiences. Conservative parents can foster empathy by actively seeking to understand their children's beliefs and values. By stepping outside their own conservative mindset and genuinely listening to their children's perspectives, parents can cultivate empathy and strengthen their bond.

Effective questioning is a valuable tool in encouraging open and constructive dialogue. By using open-ended and non-judgmental questions, conservative parents can create an environment that promotes sharing and understanding. Examples of effective questions include asking about their children's experiences, goals, and aspirations. Through thoughtful questioning, conservative parents can uncover underlying concerns and foster authentic conversations.

Non-verbal communication plays a crucial role in conveying messages and emotions. Conservative parents must be aware of their body language, facial expressions, and tone of voice, as these non-verbal cues can significantly impact conversations. By enhancing their non-verbal communication skills, conservative parents can create a more positive and welcoming atmosphere, encouraging their non-conservative children to express themselves more freely.

Emotional intelligence is essential in bridging the gap between conservative parents and non-conservative children. It requires recognizing and acknowledging emotions, both in oneself and in the other person. Conservative parents can learn to manage and express their emotions effectively by practicing active listening and using "I" statements to express their feelings without blaming or criticizing. By creating a safe environment to express emotions, conservative parents can promote honest and open communication.

Common communication pitfalls, such as making assumptions or becoming defensive, can hinder effective communication. Defensive responses, in particular, can escalate conflicts and damage relationships. Conservative parents can overcome defensiveness by engaging in self-reflection, seeking to understand their children's perspective, and reframing negative thoughts. By approaching discussions with an open mind and a willingness to understand, conservative parents can avoid defensive responses and maintain an atmosphere of constructive dialogue.

Compromise plays a pivotal role in bridging the gap between conservative parents and non-conservative children. It involves both parties being willing to find middle ground and shared values. Identifying areas of agreement and seeking mutual solutions to conflicts can help build stronger relationships based on respect and understanding. By embracing the power of compromise, conservative parents and non-conservative children can build bridges instead of deepening divides.

Trust is the cornerstone of fostering open communication within families. Conservative parents must prioritize consistent and honest communication to build trust with their non-conservative children. Honoring commitments, being transparent, and demonstrating respect and support are vital in nurturing trust. By consistently communicating openly and honestly, conservative parents can create a foundation of trust that strengthens their relationships with their children.

In some cases, communication challenges between conservative parents and non-conservative children may require professional intervention. Family therapists or mediators can provide valuable guidance and support in facilitating open dialogue and fostering understanding. Conservative parents and non-conservative children should consider seeking the assistance of qualified professionals who specialize in family communication and reconciliation.

Effective communication is the key to bridging the gap between conservative parents and their non-conservative children. By understanding and adapting to each other's communication styles, practicing active listening, and communicating with empathy and understanding, conservative parents can foster stronger relationships with their children. Avoiding communication pitfalls, seeking compromise, and building trust through consistent communication are essential for nurturing healthy dialogue. In the next segment of this book, we will explore strategies for addressing the values gap between conservative parents and non-conservative children, offering guidance on navigating this challenging terrain for the betterment of both generations and the future of conservatism.

Navigating Differences in Political Beliefs

POLITICAL BELIEFS ARE not merely opinions; they shape our individual identities, values, worldview, and self-identity.

They are deeply ingrained and contribute to how we perceive ourselves and the world around us. Understanding this profound influence is crucial in navigating differences within the family, particularly when it comes to political beliefs.

When differing political beliefs exist within a family, conflict can arise. These conflicts go beyond mere disagreements; they can strain relationships and create emotional turmoil. The clash between ideologies can lead to hurtful words, resentment, and a breakdown in communication. It is essential to recognize the emotional impact of these conflicts on family relationships and the overall well-being of the family.

Empathy is a powerful tool in understanding and accepting differing political beliefs. It allows us to step into the shoes of others and view the world from their perspective. Developing empathy for both conservative parents and their non-conservative children is crucial. It requires open-mindedness and a genuine willingness to understand the motivations and values underlying their differing beliefs.

In order to effectively navigate conversations about political beliefs within the family, certain strategies can be employed. Active listening, respect, and a non-judgmental attitude are vital in creating an atmosphere of productive discussion. Both conservative parents and non-conservative children should be encouraged to express their viewpoints and engage in respectful dialogue. By doing so, understanding and acceptance can be fostered, even if agreement is not reached.

Bridging the values gap between conservative parents and non-conservative children can be challenging. However, it is essential to find common ground and identify shared values that transcend political beliefs. Through open-mindedness and a willingness to explore shared values, both parties can work towards greater understanding and connection.

Trust and connection can be strained due to differing political beliefs. Rebuilding trust requires honest and respectful communication. Conservative parents must create a safe space for their children to express themselves without fear of judgment. They must also show a genuine interest in understanding and supporting their children's beliefs and aspirations. Foster a sense of connection, understanding, and support within the family by actively listening and validating the experiences and emotions of each family member.

Conservative parents can take proactive steps towards personal growth and self-reflection. Developing self-awareness, emotional intelligence, and empathy can significantly improve their relationships with their non-conservative children. Engaging in personal growth exercises and practices such as journaling, meditation, and seeking diverse perspectives can aid in strengthening family relationships.

Reconnecting with non-conservative children requires patience, forgiveness, and ongoing communication. Both parties must be willing to let go of past grievances and move forward in rebuilding relationships. By navigating political differences with understanding and respect, there is an opportunity for stronger and more fulfilling relationships.

Navigating differences in political beliefs within the family requires a commitment to open-mindedness, empathy, and effective communication. By understanding the influence of political beliefs on personal identities, actively engaging in respectful dialogue, and seeking common ground, conservative parents can bridge the gap with their non-conservative children. The next segment of this book will delve into strategies for addressing the values gap between conservative parents and non-conservative children, providing guidance on navigating this challenging terrain for the betterment of both generations and the future of conservatism.

The Importance of Empathy and Understanding

IN TODAY'S POLARIZED society, it has become increasingly challenging for conservative parents to maintain open and loving relationships with their non-conservative adult children. The ideological gap between generations seems to be widening, with political beliefs often causing tension and discord within families. However, amidst this divide, there lies an opportunity to heal and strengthen these fractured relationships through the powerful tools of empathy and understanding. By embracing empathy and seeking to understand the perspectives and experiences of their non-conservative children, conservative parents can bridge the gap that separates them and forge a deeper connection.

Empathy, the ability to understand and share the feelings of another, holds tremendous power when it comes to building stronger relationships. As conservative parents, we must recognize that our non-conservative children have their own unique set of experiences, values, and dreams that shape their worldview. To truly understand them, we must strive to put ourselves in their shoes. By immersing ourselves in their world, we create an opportunity for empathy to flourish. This empathetic understanding paves the way for deeper connections and bridges the gap that our differing political ideologies may have created.

Understanding is the backbone of any strong relationship. In the context of navigating differences in political beliefs between conservative parents and non-conservative children, understanding plays a pivotal role in fostering better communication and mutual respect. By taking the time to understand the values, beliefs, and experiences that shape our non-conservative children's perspectives, we can engage in meaningful conversations that transcend political arguments. This understanding allows us to communicate with empathy and respect, knowing that our intention is not to change their minds but rather to build bridges of understanding.

Understanding the challenges conservative parents face in understanding their non-conservative children is crucial to fostering empathy and bridging the gap. We must acknowledge the stark differences in upbringing that have shaped our children's belief systems and political ideologies. As conservative parents, we have likely raised our children with certain values and principles that may clash with their own evolving worldview. It is understandable that these differences can create division. However, it is precisely within this division that empathy and understanding become imperative. By recognizing the impact of these differences and seeking to understand rather than to judge, we can begin the journey towards reconciliation and transformation.

Effective communication is the lifeblood of any healthy relationship. When it comes to bridging the gap between conservative parents and non-conservative children, empathy and understanding play a vital role in creating a safe space for open and honest communication. Actively listening to our non-conservative children's thoughts, concerns, and fears allows us to validate their emotions and demonstrate our empathy. By creating this safe space, we enable them to express themselves honestly, knowing that they are heard and understood, even if we may not agree with their viewpoints. This type of communication builds trust and cultivates an environment where our non-conservative children feel valued and accepted for who they are.

Difficult conversations and disagreements are inevitable when navigating political differences within the family. Empathy and understanding serve as guiding lights in these challenging moments. Instead of approaching these conversations with judgment or a desire to assert our own beliefs, we can choose empathy as our compass. By actively listening, acknowledging our differences without judgment, and seeking common ground, we create a space for constructive dialogue. We may find that beneath the surface of our differing political ideologies, there are shared values and aspirations that can serve as a catalyst for understanding and growth. Through empathy, we can transform these difficult conversations into opportunities for connection and mutual growth.

The long-term benefits of practicing empathy and understanding within the context of conservative parents' relationships with their non-conservative children are profound. As trust grows, connections deepen, and a sense of belonging is nurtured, both generations can feel valued and respected. For our non-conservative children, knowing that they are seen, heard, and understood by their conservative parents creates a profound sense of validation and acceptance. As conservative parents, we can witness the transformative power of empathy and understanding in our relationships, building not only stronger connections with our children but also a stronger and more united family.

Developing empathy and understanding is a lifelong journey that requires intention and practice. We can take proactive steps towards this growth by cultivating habits that foster empathy and broaden our understanding of the world. Engaging in active listening, where we genuinely focus on understanding rather than responding, allows us to build stronger connections with our non-conservative children. Practicing empathy exercises, such as reflecting on our children's experiences and imagining their emotions, helps us develop a deeper understanding of their perspectives. Seeking out diverse perspectives, whether through reading or engaging in conversations with individuals who hold different beliefs, broadens our horizons and challenges our assumptions. These strategies are a key part of expanding our empathy and understanding.

As conservative parents, it is understandable that there may be skepticism or resistance towards practicing empathy and understanding. Fears of compromising one's beliefs or being seen as "weak" may arise. However, it is essential to recognize that embracing empathy and understanding does not mean sacrificing our principles or compromising our own values. On the contrary, it opens the door to meaningful conversations and the potential for growth and transformation within our relationships. By reassessing the misconceptions and fears that may hinder us from embracing empathy and understanding, we can embark on a path towards stronger and more fulfilling relationships with our non-conservative children.

Practicing empathy and understanding is not a one-time endeavor but a continuous process that requires ongoing effort, patience, and open-mindedness. Just as our political beliefs and perspectives evolve over time, so too must our empathy and understanding. We must be committed to growth, constantly seeking to deepen our understanding of our non-conservative children and their experiences. Ongoing practice and maintenance of empathy ensure that our relationships remain strong and resilient, even in the face of political differences. It is through this commitment to continuous growth that we can cultivate lasting connections, built on a foundation of empathy and understanding.

Embracing Change and Growth

AS CONSERVATIVE PARENTS, we often find ourselves rooted in our beliefs and values, resistant to change and growth. However, when it comes to our relationships with our non-conservative children, understanding plays a pivotal role in fostering better communication and mutual respect. By taking the time to understand the values, beliefs, and experiences that shape our non-conservative children's perspectives, we can engage in meaningful conversations that transcend political arguments. This understanding allows us to communicate with empathy and respect, knowing that our intention is not to change their minds but rather to build bridges of understanding.

Understanding the challenges conservative parents face in understanding their non-conservative children is crucial to fostering empathy and bridging the gap. We must acknowledge the stark differences in upbringing that have shaped our children's belief systems and political ideologies. As conservative parents, we have likely raised our children with certain values and principles that may clash with their own evolving worldview. It is understandable that these differences can create division. However, it is precisely within this division that empathy and understanding become imperative. By recognizing the impact of these differences and seeking to understand rather than to judge, we can begin the journey towards reconciliation and transformation.

Effective communication is the lifeblood of any healthy relationship. When it comes to bridging the gap between conservative parents and non-conservative children, empathy and understanding play a vital role in creating a safe space for open and honest communication. Actively listening to our non-conservative children's thoughts, concerns, and fears allows us to validate their emotions and demonstrate our empathy. By creating this safe space, we enable them to express themselves honestly, knowing that they are heard and understood, even if we may not agree with their viewpoints. This type of communication builds trust and cultivates an environment where our non-conservative children feel valued and accepted for who they are.

Difficult conversations and disagreements are inevitable when navigating political differences within the family. Empathy and understanding serve as guiding lights in these challenging moments. Instead of approaching these conversations with judgment or a desire to assert our own beliefs, we can choose empathy as our compass. By actively listening, acknowledging our differences without judgment, and seeking common ground, we create a space for constructive dialogue. We may find that beneath the surface of our differing political ideologies, there are shared values and aspirations that can serve as a catalyst for understanding and growth. Through empathy, we can transform these difficult conversations into opportunities for connection and mutual growth.

The long-term benefits of practicing empathy and understanding within the context of conservative parents' relationships with their non-conservative children are profound. As trust grows, connections deepen, and a sense of belonging is nurtured, both generations can feel valued and respected. For our non-conservative children, knowing that they are seen, heard, and understood by their conservative parents creates a profound sense of validation and acceptance. As conservative parents, we can witness the transformative power of empathy and understanding in our relationships, building not only stronger connections with our children but also a stronger and more united family.

Developing empathy and understanding is a lifelong journey that requires intention and practice. We can take proactive steps towards this growth by cultivating habits that foster empathy and broaden our understanding of the world. Engaging in active listening, where we genuinely focus on understanding rather than responding, allows us to build stronger connections with our non-conservative children. Practicing empathy exercises, such as reflecting on our children's experiences and imagining their emotions, helps us develop a deeper understanding of their perspectives. Seeking out diverse perspectives, whether through reading or engaging in conversations with individuals who hold different beliefs, broadens our horizons and challenges our assumptions. These strategies are a key part of expanding our empathy and understanding.

As conservative parents, it is understandable that there may be skepticism or resistance towards practicing empathy and understanding. Fears of compromising one's beliefs or being seen as "weak" may arise. However, it is essential to recognize that embracing empathy and understanding does not mean sacrificing our principles or compromising our own values. On the contrary, it opens the door to meaningful conversations and the potential for growth and transformation within our relationships. By reassessing the misconceptions and fears that may hinder us from embracing empathy and understanding, we can embark on a path towards stronger and more fulfilling relationships with our non-conservative children.

Practicing empathy and understanding is not a one-time endeavor but a continuous process that requires ongoing effort, patience, and open-mindedness. Just as our political beliefs and perspectives evolve over time, so too must our empathy and understanding. We must be committed to growth, constantly seeking to deepen our understanding of our non-conservative children and their experiences. Ongoing practice and maintenance of empathy ensure that our relationships remain strong and resilient, even in the face of political differences. It is through this commitment to continuous growth that we can cultivate lasting connections, built on a foundation of empathy and understanding.

Chapter 2: Examining Parenting Styles

Authoritarian Vs. Authoritative Parenting

In this segment, I want to delve deep into the topic of authoritarian versus authoritative parenting. These two styles have significant implications for the parent-child relationship, and understanding their effects is crucial for conservatives seeking to bridge the communication gap with their children.

Authoritarian parenting is often characterized by strict rules, high demands, and little room for negotiation. In an authoritarian household, obedience is paramount, and children are expected to comply without question. While this approach may initially lead to a sense of control and discipline, it can also stifle creativity and independent thinking. Children raised in an authoritarian environment may become followers rather than critical thinkers, as they are conditioned to adhere to established norms and resist questioning authority.

In contrast, authoritative parenting strikes a balance between setting boundaries and promoting open communication and autonomy. It is also important to explore the relationship between children's development and their parenting environment. Those raised in an authoritarian household may conform to societal expectations and display obedience, yet they may lack the ability to think critically and entertain alternative viewpoints. In contrast, children raised in an authoritative environment are more likely to develop independence, consider multiple perspectives, and engage in critical thinking. This allows them to navigate complex societal issues with empathy and open-mindedness.

The impact of parenting styles on receptiveness to different perspectives is significant. Authoritarian parenting, with its emphasis on conformity and rigid mindset, may limit children's receptiveness to alternative viewpoints. It reinforces a closed mentality that resists new ideas and alternative ways of thinking. On the other hand, authoritative parenting fosters an environment of open-mindedness, empathy, and constructive dialogue. This not only enhances the child's ability to empathize with diverse perspectives but also encourages thoughtful analysis and mutual understanding.

Effective communication plays a crucial role in shaping children's receptiveness to different perspectives. Authoritarian parenting often hinders open dialogue, as children may fear expressing divergent thoughts or opinions. This lack of communication creates a barrier that limits children's receptiveness to alternative viewpoints. In contrast, authoritative parenting encourages respectful and empathetic communication, allowing children to express themselves freely. This open line of communication fosters understanding, strengthens relationships, and prepares children to encounter diverse perspectives in the outside world.

Transitioning from an authoritarian to an authoritative parenting style can be challenging for parents. It requires a willingness to shift from a rigid approach to a more nurturing and open environment. Parents can start by gradually introducing opportunities for their children to express their thoughts and opinions without fear of judgment or punishment. Active listening and validation of their experiences are crucial in building trust and encouraging dialogue. Additionally, parents can promote critical thinking by encouraging their children to ask questions and explore different viewpoints.

Recognizing the importance of adaptability is also paramount. Each child has unique needs and may respond differently to parenting styles. It is essential for parents to be flexible and adaptable, adjusting their approach according to their child's developmental and emotional needs. A one-size-fits-all parenting style is unlikely to be effective in fostering receptiveness to different perspectives.

Understanding the effects of parenting styles on children's development and receptiveness to different perspectives is essential for conservatives seeking to bridge the communication gap with their children. Authoritarian parenting may lead to conformity and resistance to alternative viewpoints, while authoritative parenting promotes independence and critical thinking. By prioritizing open communication and adaptability, parents can create an environment that nurtures their children's receptiveness to diverse perspectives and strengthen their bond. It is time for conservatives to reflect on their own parenting style and consider the profound impact it may have on their relationship with their non-conservative children.

The Role of Parental Expectations

AS PARENTS, EXPECTATIONS shape not only our children's behavior but also the dynamics of our relationship with them. The expectations we hold for our children are a powerful force that can influence their choices, actions, and even their willingness to engage in open dialogue with us. It is crucial that we understand the impact of our expectations and how they can either enhance or hinder our connection with our children.

Parental expectations can be defined as the standards or goals that we set for our children. They can vary from parent to parent, influenced by factors such as cultural background, personal beliefs, and individual experiences. These expectations can take different forms, ranging from academic and career aspirations to behavioral and moral standards.

The influence of parental expectations on our children's behavior is profound. From a young age, children may feel the weight of our expectations, often believing that meeting these expectations is vital for gaining our approval and acceptance. This pressure to conform can lead to behaviors aimed at meeting our standards, but it can also stifle their ability to develop their own identities and explore their true passions and interests.

In addition to influencing behavior, parental expectations can also impact communication within the parent-child relationship. Children may be hesitant to express their true thoughts and feelings if they fear judgment or disappointment from us. They may withhold their opinions, avoid discussing certain topics, or even withdraw from engaging in conversations altogether. When our expectations become a barrier to open dialogue, it becomes increasingly difficult to understand and connect with our children.

The way we communicate with our children plays a significant role in shaping our expectations of them. If our communication style is open, supportive, and non-judgmental, we are more likely to have healthy and realistic expectations. However, if our communication is judgmental, controlling, or dismissive, we may unknowingly set unrealistic and damaging expectations that are not in line with our children's individual needs and abilities.

To overcome the negative effects of parental expectations, it is crucial that we create a supportive and non-judgmental environment that encourages open dialogue. This means actively listening to our children, valuing their perspectives, and refraining from imposing our beliefs onto them. We must allow our children to develop their own identities and express themselves freely, even if their thoughts and choices may differ from what we had initially expected.

Building a foundation of trust and respect is essential in fostering open communication. By demonstrating unconditional love and acceptance towards our children, regardless of whether they meet our expectations or not, we create a safe and supportive environment for them to freely express themselves. It is through trust and respect that we can truly connect with our children and establish a meaningful dialogue.

As parents, we must also be willing to adjust our expectations as our children grow and change. Each child is unique, with their own strengths, weaknesses, and interests. It is important to set individualized expectations that are realistic and considerate of our children's abilities and aspirations. Being flexible and adaptable in our expectations is key to nurturing a positive and healthy parent-child relationship.

Ultimately, the role of parental expectations in our relationship with our children is powerful and far-reaching. It is up to us to reflect on our own parenting style and make the necessary adjustments to foster open dialogue and understanding. By embracing open communication, encouraging independence and self-expression, and demonstrating unconditional love, we can bridge the communication gap and build a stronger connection with our children.

Balancing Discipline and Freedom

GROWING UP IN A CONSERVATIVE household, where discipline reigned supreme, I can understand the significance of finding the right balance between discipline and freedom in the parent-child relationship. It is not an easy task to navigate the fine line between strict rules and allowing children the freedom to express themselves and develop their thoughts and opinions. However, I have come to realize that this balance is crucial for nurturing a healthy and open environment where children can truly flourish.

Discipline, in its essence, entails consistent guidance, structure, and rules. It provides a sense of security and teaches children about boundaries and consequences. It is through discipline that children learn valuable life skills such as self-control, responsibility, and respect for authority. As parents, it is our duty to provide this guidance and structure for our children, setting clear expectations for their behavior and holding them accountable when needed.

My father ruled with an iron fist. I was not "allowed" to register as a Democrat or Communist or any other party except for the Grand Old Party. He even went with me to the place where I signed up initially. As soon as I could, I filed a Change of Party request. Today, in North Carolina, my voter card says, NPA. No Party Affiliation.

On the other hand, it is equally important to recognize the need for freedom. Allowing children to explore their individuality and develop their own thoughts and opinions is essential for their personal growth. A lack of freedom can stifle creativity and hinder the development of critical thinking skills. As conservative parents, it can be challenging to give our children the freedom to think independently, especially when their thoughts may differ from our own. However, by allowing them the space to explore their individuality, we foster an environment that encourages personal growth and the formation of a strong sense of self.

While discipline and freedom both hold value on their own, extreme measures can be detrimental to the parent-child relationship. Excessive discipline can lead to rebellion, resentment, and a breakdown in communication. When children feel suffocated by strict rules and constant control, they may withdraw and refuse to engage with us. On the other hand, excessive freedom, without adequate guidance and boundaries, can result in a lack of responsibility and a disregard for authority. This can be equally damaging, causing children to spiral out of control and potentially harm themselves or others.

The key lies in finding the middle ground, striking a balance between discipline and freedom. This delicate equilibrium requires us to set age-appropriate boundaries while also allowing room for open communication, mutual respect, and the development of critical thinking skills. It is important to create an environment where our children feel safe to express their thoughts and opinions, even if they differ from our own. By nurturing independent thinking, we encourage our children to become well-rounded individuals who can confidently navigate the complexities of the world.

In order to strike this balance, we must build trust and mutual understanding with our children. This requires actively listening to them, validating their feelings, and finding compromises when conflicts arise. It is essential to create a safe and non-judgmental space for dialogue and respectful disagreement. By demonstrating our unconditional love and acceptance, even in moments of disagreement, we strengthen our bond with our children and foster a deeper connection.

Respecting our children's individuality is paramount in this journey. It is crucial for us, as conservative parents, to embrace and celebrate our children's unique identities and perspectives, even if they differ from our own conservative values. Allowing freedom of thought and expression can lead to deeper connections and a stronger parent-child relationship where differences are acknowledged and respected.

However, finding the balance between discipline and freedom is an ongoing process that may face challenges and setbacks. It requires us to be patient, adaptable, and willing to reassess our approach as our children grow and develop. Each child is unique, with their own needs, strengths, and weaknesses. As parents, we must be willing to adjust our expectations and adapt our parenting style accordingly.

Finding the balance between discipline and freedom is crucial in fostering a healthy parent-child relationship. It requires us to reflect on our own parenting style and consider how we can create an environment that promotes both boundaries and the freedom to think and express oneself. By embracing open communication, encouraging independent thinking, and demonstrating unconditional love and acceptance, we can bridge the communication gap and build a stronger connection with our children.

Fostering Mutual Respect and Trust

BUILDING A STRONG AND healthy relationship with our non-conservative children requires us to foster mutual respect and trust. This is essential in creating an environment where open dialogue can flourish and where both parties feel heard and understood. Without mutual respect and trust, conversations can quickly devolve into arguments and misunderstandings, further widening the divide between conservative parents and their non-conservative children. So, how can we foster mutual respect and trust?

First, it is important to understand and empathize with the perspectives of conservative parents. As conservatives, you hold certain beliefs and values that may differ from those of your non-conservative children. It can be challenging to comprehend why they hold their positions or why they may reject your beliefs. However, in order to bridge this gap, you must approach their perspectives with empathy and curiosity. By genuinely trying to understand their viewpoints, we can lay the groundwork for productive and respectful conversations.

Your life is not your child's life. They have seen things in their life you have not. Since 1980, there have been so many wars, crises, economic conundrums, missiles, bombs, death, destruction, and mayhem, all shown on the news 24/7. It is so easy to see what is causing our current generations to become less conservative, that conservatives are the enemy, because we see what they are doing to the US and to the world.

Similarly, it is crucial to understand the perspectives of our non-conservative children. They may view our conservative beliefs as restrictive, outdated, or even harmful. It is important for us to listen to their concerns and validate their experiences, even if we may not fully agree with their conclusions. By showing open-mindedness and respect, we can create an atmosphere where they feel safe to express themselves and engage in meaningful discussions.

Creating an environment of open dialogue is essential in fostering mutual respect and trust. This means setting aside our preconceived notions or judgments and actively listening to our children without interruption or defensiveness. We must ensure that they feel heard and valued, even if we disagree with them. It is important to avoid personal attacks or dismissive remarks during conversations, as these can escalate tensions and impede progress.

Practicing empathy in communication is another powerful tool in building mutual respect and trust. This involves actively trying to understand and appreciate the emotions and perspectives of our non-conservative children. By acknowledging and validating their experiences, we send the message that their feelings and ideas are important to us. This can lead to deeper connections and a greater understanding of each other's viewpoints. I have gone over this before. Empathy is important. Understand your children, even if you do not agree with them. This would go so far. Do not use every interaction to mention something Biden or some other political person you dislike has done to wrong you.

Identifying shared values and interests can serve as a foundation for mutual respect and trust. While our political beliefs may differ, there are often common values that we can find and celebrate. Engaging in activities or topics that we both enjoy can help create a sense of unity and shared experiences. By focusing on these commonalities, we can foster a sense of connection and respect that transcends our political differences.

Building trust requires transparency and honesty. We must be open and authentic in our communication with our non-conservative children. This means sharing our own stories and experiences, even if they relate to our conservative beliefs. By being vulnerable, we show that we trust them with our truths, and this can encourage them to do the same. Building trust takes time, consistency, and a willingness to be vulnerable.

Conflict is inevitable in any relationship, including the one between conservative parents and non-conservative children. However, it is important to approach conflicts in a constructive and respectful manner. This means actively seeking resolution and compromise rather than engaging in personal attacks or trying to prove one's point. Conflict resolution techniques, such as active listening, perspective-taking, and finding common ground, can help navigate disagreements and foster understanding.

Respecting boundaries and differences is crucial in maintaining mutual respect and trust. As conservative parents, we must acknowledge and respect our children's individuality, even if it differs from our own beliefs. By setting boundaries that promote mutual respect and understanding, we create an environment where both parties feel safe to express themselves and pursue their own interests. Boundaries should be negotiated and agreed upon, taking into consideration the needs and values of all involved.

Nurturing a supportive network can also aid in fostering mutual respect and trust. Seeking guidance and understanding from like-minded individuals or support groups can provide a sense of validation and support during challenging times. It is important to surround ourselves with positive influences who can provide insight and perspective from both sides of the spectrum.

Committing to continuous growth and learning is essential in maintaining a healthy relationship with our non-conservative children. This means actively seeking out opportunities for personal development and education. Attending workshops, reading books, or engaging in dialogues with experts in communication and understanding can provide valuable insights and tools for navigating the complexities of our relationship.

Finally, it is important to celebrate the journey of mutual respect and trust. Building a strong relationship with our non-conservative children takes time, effort, and dedication.

By acknowledging and celebrating the milestones and successes along the way, we create a positive and reinforcing cycle that strengthens our bond. Sharing success stories of conservative parents and non-conservative children who have overcome their differences can serve as inspiration and motivation for our own journey.

Fostering mutual respect and trust between conservative parents and non-conservative children is crucial in building stronger relationships. By understanding and empathizing with each other's perspectives, creating an environment of open dialogue, practicing empathy in communication, identifying shared values, and interests, building trust through transparency and honesty, resolving conflicts constructively, recognizing boundaries and respecting differences, nurturing a supportive network, committing to continuous growth and learning, and celebrating the journey, we can bridge the gap and create a foundation of mutual respect and trust that allows for meaningful conversations and deeper connections.

Adapting Parenting Approaches

AS CONSERVATIVE PARENTS, it is essential to recognize the need for adapting your parenting approaches in order to better connect with your adult children. The generation gap that often exists between you and your non-conservative children can create strain in your relationship, making it imperative that we reflect on your current parenting style and consider whether it aligns with the unique needs and values of your adult children.

One way to adapt our parenting approach is by understanding and acknowledging the perspectives of your adult children. It is crucial to engage in open and non-judgmental conversations with them, listening and trying to gain insight into their experiences. By actively trying to understand and appreciate their emotions and worldviews, we send the message that their feelings and ideas are important to us. This can lead to deeper connections and a greater understanding of each other's viewpoints.

Flexibility and open-mindedness are also key in adapting our parenting strategies. As our adult children grow and develop their own identities, it is important for us to be flexible in accommodating their changing needs and values. This might involve being more supportive of their career choices, even if they differ from our expectations, or embracing diverse relationships that challenge our traditional beliefs. By adapting our parenting strategies to meet their needs, we show them that we respect their autonomy and independence.

Finding common ground is another important aspect of adapting our parenting approach. While our political or social beliefs may differ from those of our adult children, it is possible to identify shared values and interests that can serve as a foundation for mutual respect and trust. Engaging in activities or topics that we both enjoy can help create a sense of unity and shared experiences. By focusing on these commonalities, we can foster a sense of connection and respect that transcends our political differences.

Respecting the autonomy and independence of our adult children is crucial in adapting our parenting approach. It is important for us to let go of control and allow our children to make their own decisions. By doing so, we show them that we trust their judgment and respect their ability to navigate their own lives. This can lead to a healthier and more balanced relationship, built on mutual respect and understanding.

It is also valuable for conservative parents to learn from non-conservative parenting approaches. By being open to different perspectives and incorporating elements of other parenting styles, we can better meet the needs of our adult children. This may involve considering alternative methods of communication, discipline, or problem-solving that may be more effective in bridging the gap between us and our non-conservative children.

Building a strong relationship with our adult children takes time, effort, and patience. It is important to approach this journey with a positive attitude and a commitment to the process. There may be challenges and setbacks along the way, but by staying persistent and remaining open to growth and learning, we can continue to improve and strengthen our parent-child relationship.

Adapting our parenting approaches is essential in building stronger relationships with our non-conservative adult children. By recognizing the need for flexibility, understanding their perspectives, finding common ground, respecting their autonomy, learning from other parenting approaches, and remaining patient and persistent, we can bridge the gap and create a foundation of mutual respect and trust that allows for meaningful conversations and deeper connections.

Chapter 3: Overcoming Polarization and Division

Recognizing the Impact of Polarization

Political polarization has crept its way into the very fabric of our lives, even infiltrating our most sacred bonds - those within the family. As conservatives, we often find ourselves at odds with our non-conservative children, bringing about strained relationships and emotional distance. The division is rooted in the clash of political ideologies, with each side becoming entrenched in their beliefs. This chapter aims to shed light on the far-reaching consequences of this polarization within families and offers a path towards healing and understanding.

The emotional toll that political polarization takes on family members cannot be understated. Frustration, anger, and hurt can become constant companions in the presence of opposing political beliefs. The ones we love, our own flesh and blood, seem so distant when we are unable to find common ground. Our minds and hearts bear the weight of these negative emotions, resulting in a decline in overall well-being and mental health. Sleepless nights, anxious thoughts, and strained interactions become the norm, leaving us questioning what went wrong and why our children won't talk to us.

WHY WON'T MY CHILDREN TALK TO ME? A BOOK FOR CONSERVATIVES

Political polarization slowly erodes the foundation of effective communication within families. Rational discussions turn into fiery arguments, where tempers flare and words are wielded as weapons. Listening to one another becomes increasingly challenging, with each side struggling to understand and empathize with the perspectives of the other. Instead of seeking understanding, we often find ourselves locked in a cycle of point-counterpoint, unable to bridge the divide that separates us.

Once political polarization firmly takes hold within a family, a sense of isolation and disconnection permeates the air. Family gatherings and once joyous occasions can quickly turn tense and uncomfortable, with individuals opting to avoid or withdraw from interactions altogether. This self-imposed isolation takes a toll on the dynamics that should have been the bedrock of our family life. The laughter and love that once characterized family moments now seem like distant memories, replaced by a cavernous void that only grows wider with time.

The impact of political polarization within families extends far beyond the present moment. These negative dynamics and strained relationships have the potential to seep into the lives of our children and grandchildren, turning polarization into a self-perpetuating cycle within the family unit. If left unaddressed, such division may rob future generations of the opportunity to experience the deep bonds and support that should come from family ties. It is incumbent upon us to break this cycle and foster healthier relationships for the well-being and unity of our loved ones yet to come.

The toll that political polarization takes on the mental health of individuals cannot be ignored. Stress, anxiety, and depression often increase as our own political beliefs are viewed as a threat or a source of division within our own family. The constant feeling of being attacked or marginalized leads individuals to question their self-worth and their place within the family unit. Coping strategies and support become vital tools in navigating the minefield of political polarization. We must take care to protect our mental well-being and find ways to seek solace amidst the chaos.

Trust and respect, foundational elements of any healthy relationship, erode with the presence of differing political beliefs. The very fabric of our familial bonds begins to unravel as this erosion takes hold. Once fractured, rebuilding trust and respect becomes a herculean task, requiring patience, understanding, and intentional effort. It is through a commitment to creating a safe space for dialogue and mutual respect that we can hope to mend the wounds inflicted by political polarization.

Political polarization can all too easily overshadow other important aspects of family life. We become consumed by our disagreements, losing sight of the love and connection that should guide our interactions. Our relationships become distorted, emphasized solely by the political lens through which we view one another. It is essential to prioritize the preservation of family relationships over political differences, placing love and acceptance before ideology.

The long-term implications of political polarization on family unity are profound. Without intervention, divisions and polarization can fracture the family structure, leading to alienation and a breakdown in communication. Estrangement becomes a real risk, and what should be a source of support and unconditional love may turn into a source of stress and conflict. Families may find it increasingly difficult to come together for life events, holidays, or even routine gatherings, as the tension becomes too difficult to navigate.

Yet, it's worth noting that confronting these challenges head-on can also offer an opportunity for growth and greater understanding within the family. Addressing differing political views doesn't necessarily have to lead to discord; it can also lead to a richer, more nuanced perspective of the world and each other. By practicing empathy, active listening, and open dialogue, we can learn to appreciate the complexity of the views held by our family members, even if we don't agree with them.

While political polarization poses a significant threat to family unity, it also presents an opportunity for transformation and growth. The key lies in how we choose to address these differences. Through proactive steps like fostering a safe space for discussion, prioritizing the emotional health of the family, and remaining committed to the values of love and respect, we can hope to mitigate the damaging effects of political polarization and preserve the integrity of our familial bonds.

Building Bridges, Not Walls

IN ORDER TO BUILD BRIDGES between conservative parents and their non-conservative children, it is crucial to first understand the root causes of their differences. This requires a genuine sense of open-mindedness and a willingness to learn about each other's perspectives. It involves recognizing that these differences stem from a myriad of factors such as upbringing, personal experiences, and the influence of the broader society. By acknowledging and delving into these underlying sources of divergence, we can begin to foster a deeper understanding and appreciation for our loved ones' unique viewpoints.

One of the most significant steps towards building bridges is engaging in open and honest communication. This means actively listening to our non-conservative children without judgment, truly seeking to understand their thoughts and feelings. It requires setting aside our preconceived notions and biases, and being willing to learn from their experiences. Additionally, expressing our own emotions and thoughts in a respectful manner allows for a constructive dialogue that can bridge the gap between our differing beliefs.

Empathy is the cornerstone of building bridges with non-conservative children, as it allows us to foster understanding and connection across the divide. Cultivating empathy involves putting ourselves in their shoes, striving to see the world through their eyes. It requires seeking common ground and acknowledging the validity of their perspectives, even if we do not fully agree. By approaching conversations with empathy, we create an atmosphere of acceptance and understanding, laying the foundation for deeper connection and reconciliation.

Finding common ground between conservative parents and their non-conservative children is essential in bridging the divide. While it may seem difficult at first, there are always shared values, interests, and activities that can serve as a bridge for understanding and connection. By actively seeking out these areas of overlap, we can create opportunities for meaningful interaction and dialogue that transcend our political differences. This shared space allows us to build a sense of unity and strengthens the bonds that hold our family together.

In the midst of political polarization, it is crucial to acknowledge and validate the emotions of our non-conservative children. It is important to create a safe space where they feel heard and understood, even if their views differ from our own. By genuinely listening and providing validation, we foster an environment where they feel valued and acknowledged. This enables us to establish stronger connections and rebuild trust, even amid political disagreements.

Respecting boundaries is paramount in building bridges with non-conservative children. It is essential to navigate discussions without crossing boundaries or imposing our beliefs on them. It involves recognizing when to step back and allow for personal autonomy, considering their independence as adults with their own unique perspectives. By respecting their boundaries, we convey our willingness to create a balanced and respectful relationship built on trust and mutual understanding.

In some cases, seeking professional help, such as family therapy or counseling, can be a valuable tool in bridging the gap between conservative parents and their non-conservative children. These professionals specialize in family dynamics and communication and can provide guidance and support tailored to our specific situation. By engaging in therapy or counseling, we demonstrate our commitment to healing and rebuilding our relationships, ensuring that we have the necessary resources to navigate the complexities of political polarization within the family.

The journey of building bridges with non-conservative children requires patience and persistence. It is crucial to remain committed to the process, even in the face of setbacks or challenges. Patience and persistence enable us to weather the storm of political differences, allowing for growth and understanding over time. By staying steadfast in our efforts, we can create an environment of trust and mutual respect that fosters stronger bonds within the family unit.

As we strive to build bridges, it is important to not only tolerate but celebrate the differences between conservative parents and non-conservative children. Embracing diversity and appreciating the unique perspectives each individual brings to the table can lead to a deeper understanding and connection. By seeking common ground while respecting and valuing our differences, we can create a more harmonious and inclusive family dynamic.

Engaging in self-reflection is vital for conservative parents as they navigate the process of building bridges with their non-conservative children. Taking the time to understand our own beliefs, motivations, and biases allows us to approach conversations with a greater sense of self-awareness. By reflecting on our perspectives and challenging our own assumptions, we can foster an environment of growth and learning, leading to enhanced empathy and understanding.

Sharing personal stories and experiences can be a powerful way to connect with non-conservative children. By authentically sharing our own perspectives, emotions, and journeys, we create opportunities for deeper empathy and understanding. Personal storytelling allows us to bridge the gap between political differences, revealing our shared humanity and the common threads that bind us together as a family.

Patience, love, and unconditional support are essential ingredients in building bridges with non-conservative children. It is important to convey to them our unwavering love and support, even when our beliefs diverge. By demonstrating our commitment to their well-being and happiness, we create an environment that encourages openness and understanding. This foundation of love and support enables us to navigate the complexities of political polarization with grace and compassion.

Embracing change and personal growth is vital as we navigate the process of building bridges with our non-conservative children. It requires an openness to evolving beliefs and perspectives while still maintaining our core values and sense of self. By embracing change and growth, we demonstrate to our loved ones that we are willing to learn and adapt, fostering an atmosphere of growth and understanding within the family.

Finding and engaging in shared interests and activities can be a powerful way to build bridges with non-conservative children. By exploring new hobbies or participating in existing ones together, we create opportunities for meaningful connection and dialogue. Shared experiences allow for a deeper understanding of each other's passions and can serve as catalysts for building stronger family bonds.

Rebuilding trust and seeking reconciliation with non-conservative children is a process that requires patience and consistent effort. It involves acknowledging past mistakes, offering sincere apologies, and demonstrating our commitment to change and understanding. By actively working towards rebuilding trust, we create a safe space for dialogue and create the foundation for a more harmonious and empathetic relationship.

Respecting the autonomy and independence of non-conservative children is paramount in the process of building bridges. Acknowledging their agency and freedom of thought allows for a more open and respectful relationship. By empowering them to express their own beliefs and values, we allow for a greater sense of mutuality and understanding, fostering a stronger bond within the family unit.

Celebrating progress and small victories along the journey of building bridges is pivotal in maintaining motivation and fostering a sense of accomplishment. By acknowledging and appreciating the steps taken towards understanding and empathy, we reinforce the importance of continuous growth and improvement. Celebrating progress ensures that we stay invested in the process, even during challenging times.

Seeking support from like-minded communities or organizations can provide invaluable guidance and validation during the process of building bridges. These communities can offer resources, advice, and a sense of belonging, creating a network of support that bolsters our efforts. By connecting with others who have gone through similar experiences, we gain strength and resilience, ensuring that we do not navigate this journey alone.

Building bridges with non-conservative children is an ongoing journey that requires commitment, adaptability, and a focus on long-term goals. It is important to recognize that understanding and empathy are not achieved overnight but are cultivated through consistent effort. By embracing this journey with openness and a willingness to learn, we create a future filled with deeper connections, stronger bonds, and a renewed sense of unity within our families.

The Role of Technology and Social Media

IN TODAY'S DIGITAL era, technology and social media have become interwoven into the fabric of society, shaping cultural narratives and influencing political discourse. As conservative parents, it is crucial we acknowledge and understand the role these digital forces play in impacting political divides within families.

Social media platforms provide people with unprecedented access to create and consume content aligning with their own political perspectives. This ability to customize feeds and surround ourselves with viewpoints we agree with can reinforce "echo chambers" that validate our own beliefs while dismissing or demonizing opposing views. When conservative parents and non-conservative children occupy different digital spaces and consume disparate media, it can solidify polarization.

The anonymity and lack of face-to-face interaction online often leads to overly harsh, uncivil discourse around political issues on social media. Being exposed to constant charged rhetoric on these platforms can breed conflict and animosity among family members. It primes both sides to interpret opposing viewpoints in the worst possible light.

The algorithms and pull of social media can create dependencies, where users become consumed by outrage and controversy. When conservative parents and children obsessively engage online, it can displace real-life interactions and deepen polarization. Nuance and empathy are lost when political positions are reduced to tweets and posts.

While technology and social media are catalysts for divides, they also offer tools to bridge them. Shared online experiences, from videos to games to apps, can create positive interactions. Virtual communication can supplement face-to-face engagement. Exposure to diverse perspectives online encourages learning and growth.

As conservative parents, we must be aware of both the positives and pitfalls of technology. We cannot allow digital tools to control or define family relationships. With mindfulness, these technologies can be harnessed constructively, and their hazards mitigated through open communication, empathy and unconditional love.

Finding Common Ground

IN THE MIDST OF POLITICAL polarization and division, it is imperative to find common ground and foster connection despite our differences. As conservative parents, it is natural for us to hold strong beliefs and convictions that may differ from those of our non-conservative children. However, it is through understanding and reconciliation that we can bridge the chasm between us and build stronger relationships within our families. The goal of this segment is to explore the ways in which we can find common ground, seek mutual understanding, and promote a sense of unity that transcends our political differences.

Shared values play a significant role in bridging political differences and building connections within families. While it is easy to focus solely on our divergent beliefs, it is essential to identify and emphasize the values we hold in common. These shared values serve as a starting point for conversations and discussions, allowing us to find areas of agreement and build upon them. Compassion, fairness, and the desire for a better world are all examples of common values that can serve as foundations for deeper understanding and connection.

In addition to shared values, identifying and engaging in shared interests can foster connection and bridge the gap between conservative parents and non-conservative children. While our political beliefs may differ, there are often activities or hobbies that both sides can enjoy and participate in together. Whether it be hiking, cooking, or engaging in community service, finding common ground through shared interests opens the door to meaningful and enjoyable experiences that can strengthen relationships and deepen understanding.

the experiences and emotions of our non-conservative children without judgment or defensiveness, we demonstrate a willingness to empathize and understand their perspectives. By sharing our own personal stories and anecdotes, we can touch the hearts of our loved ones and help them see us as individuals capable of growth and change. When we lead with empathy and emotional understanding, the barriers created by politics begin to crumble, leaving space for greater connection and unity.

Active listening is a vital skill in finding common ground and fostering connection. It requires us to be present, open-minded, and truly engaged in the dialogue. By actively listening to our non-conservative children, we convey respect and value their perspectives, even if they differ from our own. This deep listening allows us to understand their concerns, fears, and hopes, paving the way for constructive conversations and a more profound appreciation of the complex individuals they have become.

Empathy lies at the heart of finding common ground and forging connections. As conservative parents, it is essential to make a genuine effort to understand and empathize with our non-conservative children's perspectives and experiences. We must be willing to put ourselves in their shoes, considering the societal and cultural influences that have shaped their beliefs. By striving for a deeper understanding of their unique journeys, we demonstrate our commitment to empathy and lay the groundwork for building a bridge of mutual understanding. Again, empathy. This is so important I am mentioning it multiple times. Understand where your children are coming from, ideologically. Even if you do not agree with their beliefs. Especially if you do not agree with their beliefs.

Open and respectful dialogue is fundamental to finding common ground and fostering connections between conservative parents and non-conservative children. It is crucial to create a safe space where everyone feels heard and respected, regardless of political beliefs. This requires setting aside preconceived notions, actively seeking to understand, and engaging in conversations free from judgment or defensiveness. By promoting open dialogue and respectful communication, we break down barriers and create an environment conducive to connection and understanding.

While our political beliefs may differ, there are often overlapping values between conservatives and non-conservatives that can serve as common ground. For example, both sides may prioritize family, education, or the pursuit of happiness. By identifying these shared values, we can build upon them and foster connection. Instead of viewing our differences as insurmountable obstacles, we can utilize our common values as bridges that lead to deeper understanding and appreciation.

Shared interests and activities provide opportunities for connection and understanding beyond political differences. By engaging in activities or initiatives that both conservatives and non-conservatives enjoy, we create shared experiences that can bring us closer together. Whether it is attending a concert, volunteering for a cause, or exploring a shared hobby, these activities allow us to see and appreciate each other as individuals with multifaceted identities beyond politics. Through shared interests, we build stronger bonds and create lasting memories that transcend the political divide.

While finding common ground is essential, it is equally important to recognize and celebrate the differences between conservative parents and non-conservative children. Embracing diversity of thought and respecting each other's unique perspectives fosters an environment of open-mindedness and acceptance. By celebrating the differences that make us who we are, we create a space in which everyone feels valued and understood. In doing so, we cultivate a sense of unity that honors and appreciates the rich tapestry of our family.

Overcoming deep-seated divisiveness and polarization within families is a daunting task. It requires a commitment to love and understand our non-conservative children unconditionally, despite our political differences. We must continually remind ourselves that our ultimate goal is to nurture relationships and ensure the well-being of our family. By grounding our interactions in love and understanding, we create a culture of openness and empathy that can bridge the divide and enable us to rebuild and strengthen our connections.

Building bridges between conservative parents and non-conservative children takes deliberate effort and intention. It involves taking practical steps to promote connection and understanding. These steps include initiating conversations, listening actively, seeking to understand, and expressing empathy. By consistently demonstrating our commitment to connection and understanding, we lay the groundwork for healing, growth, and reconciliation within the family unit.

Central to the process of finding common ground and fostering connection is the cultivation of mutual respect. Mutual respect involves acknowledging and valuing each other's perspectives, even when they differ significantly. It means considering the life experiences and beliefs that have shaped our non-conservative children's views and demonstrating an appreciation for their autonomy as independent adults. By fostering a sense of mutual respect, we create an environment of fairness, understanding, and trust that nurtures healthy relationships within the family.

Navigating the path of finding common ground with our non-conservative children requires both patience and persistence. Building bridges and mending relationships take time and effort. There will be setbacks along the way, moments of frustration, and moments of uncertainty. However, by remaining patient and persistent, we demonstrate our unwavering commitment to our loved ones and our willingness to work through challenges to achieve understanding. Patience and persistence allow for growth, empathy, and greater connection, fostering a lasting bond that transcends politics.

In the journey of finding common ground with our non-conservative children, we must remember that our goal is not to change or convert them to our political beliefs. Instead, it is about deepening our understanding, fostering empathy, and promoting a sense of unity within our families. By seeking to understand, actively listening, and embracing shared values and interests, we lay a foundation for connection and reconciliation. It is through these efforts that we can slowly bridge the gap and create an environment of respect, trust, and love that stands the test of time.

Long-term Ramifications

WHEN POLITICAL DIVISIONS arise within families, there can be a temptation to avoid rocking the boat and leave conflicts unresolved. However, allowing these rifts to become entrenched without addressing the underlying issues can have detrimental consequences over time. Failing to take action now to heal relationships can set families on a destructive course for years to come.

- Unresolved political tensions often worsen over time as resentment builds and perspectives grow more polarized through confirmation bias. Small gaps can turn into unbridgeable chasms if healthy communication and understanding are not prioritized.

- A lack of resolution creates an environment where political views become personal, making objectivity impossible. Family members may come to see each other as enemies instead of loved ones, causing lasting emotional and psychological damage.

- Without efforts to find common ground, families may stop interacting as much to avoid conflict or judgment over political differences. This can lead to isolation and estrangement, with generations growing apart rather than closer together.

- Parents may avoid sharing important values, perspectives and life lessons with their children because they fear differences in opinion. This prevents the passing down of wisdom through generations.

- In the absence of open dialogue, assumptions and misconceptions flourish, entrenching prejudice. Younger generations may unfairly associate conservatism with negativity if these perceptions go unaddressed.

• If parents appear dismissive of their children's political leanings, it may cause them to rebel and become even more polarized in their positions. They may come to define themselves primarily in opposition to their parents' views.

• A lack of mutual understanding and empathy can become normalized within families over decades, making efforts at reconciliation much more difficult. Healing requires addressing issues early before relationships are too badly damaged.

• Allowing family political tensions to solidify establishes a negative precedent for future generations. The divides we enable today may be replicated and amplified in our children and grandchildren if unresolved, risking a cycle of dysfunction.

The risks are too grave to allow political polarization to fracture families long-term. By taking action now, conservative parents can work to heal rifts through open dialogue, empathy and love—preventing permanent damage and protecting the sanctity of family.

Active Listening and Open Dialogue

IN YOUR JOURNEY TO repair and strengthen the bond with your non-conservative children, two crucial communication techniques come to the forefront: active listening and open dialogue. These techniques hold the power to bridge understanding and heal the wounds caused by political differences. Active listening involves giving our undivided attention to our children, being present in the moment, and showing empathy and understanding. Open dialogue, on the other hand, creates a safe space where both parties can express their thoughts, feelings, and perspectives without judgment or interruption. By embracing these communication techniques, we can foster connection, create understanding, and lay the foundation for a healthier parent-child relationship.

Active listening is not simply about hearing the words spoken by our non-conservative children; it is about fully engaging with them on an emotional and empathetic level. When we practice active listening, we give our undivided attention to our children, silencing the distractions that may pull us away from the present moment. We set aside our preconceived notions and biases, allowing ourselves to truly understand their perspective. By demonstrating empathy and understanding, we validate their feelings and experiences, creating a safe space for them to open up and share their thoughts and emotions without fear of judgment or dismissal. Active listening requires us to be fully present and receptive, inviting a deeper and more meaningful connection with our non-conservative children.

Active listening holds profound benefits for both the parent and the child. For the non-conservative child, the simple act of truly being heard and understood can have a transformative effect on their perception of the parent-child relationship. By actively listening to their thoughts and concerns, we communicate that their opinions are valued and respected, regardless of whether or not we agree with them. This validation creates a sense of trust, fostering a more open and honest line of communication. In turn, as parents, we gain valuable insight into our children's lives, understanding their experiences and worldview in a more profound way. Active listening allows us to bridge the gap between us and our non-conservative children, replacing conflict with understanding and fostering a stronger, more resilient relationship.

While active listening sets the stage for true understanding, open dialogue provides the framework for genuine communication and connection. Open dialogue is a process of creating a safe space where both the conservative parents and their non-conservative children can express themselves freely and honestly. It is about setting aside our predispositions and allowing room for our loved ones to share their thoughts, feelings, and perspectives. In this safe space, judgment and interruption have no place. Instead, respect and empathy prevail, opening the door for constructive conversations and mutual understanding. Open dialogue sets the stage for vulnerability, where all parties involved feel empowered to speak from the heart without fear of rejection. It is within this open dialogue that the seeds of reconciliation and growth are planted.

For non-conservative children, navigating a political divide within their own family can be incredibly challenging. They may fear expressing their thoughts, beliefs, and feelings, hesitant to engage in conversations that may lead to conflict or rejection. As conservative parents, it is crucial to create a safe space that welcomes and encourages open dialogue. By reassuring our children that their perspectives will be heard and respected, we create an environment where they can feel comfortable expressing themselves honestly and authentically. This safe space dismantles barriers and opens up channels of communication that were previously hindered. When we foster an atmosphere of trust and acceptance, our non-conservative children can speak openly, paving the way for deeper understanding and conflict resolution. Creating a safe space gives them the reassurance they need to share their experiences and viewpoints, ultimately leading to a healthier and more harmonious parent-child relationship.

Active listening serves as a guiding force in the practice of open dialogue, providing the tools necessary to facilitate meaningful conversations. Through active listening techniques, such as paraphrasing, asking open-ended questions, and reflecting emotions, we can encourage our non-conservative children to share their thoughts and experiences more openly. Paraphrasing allows us to restate their words in our own language, ensuring that we have understood them correctly and emphasizing our commitment to truly hearing them. Asking open-ended questions invites them to expand upon their thoughts and delve deeper into their perspective. By reflecting their emotions, we validate their feelings and demonstrate empathy, showing them that we are deeply invested in understanding their experiences. Active listening techniques not only pave the way for a more productive conversation but also foster a sense of safety within the dialogue, encouraging our non-conservative children to express themselves without reservation.

Healing Wounds and Rebuilding Relationships

IN THE JOURNEY OF HEALING wounds and rebuilding relationships, one of the most powerful tools we have at our disposal is forgiveness. Forgiveness is a remarkable concept that transcends mere acceptance or understanding. It is the act of letting go of resentment and choosing to release the emotional burden that comes with holding onto past grievances. When we forgive, we free ourselves from the chains of anger and bitterness, allowing healing and reconciliation to take place.

Forgiveness is not about condoning or forgetting the hurtful actions of our non-conservative children. It is about recognizing that holding onto anger and resentment only perpetuates the cycle of pain and further drives a wedge between us. By choosing to forgive, we open ourselves up to the possibility of rebuilding the fractured relationship with our children. It requires a genuine willingness to let go of the past and move forward with an open heart.

Through forgiveness, we also set an example for our non-conservative children. We show them that forgiveness is a strength, not a weakness, and that it is possible to transcend political differences and find common ground. By extending forgiveness, we create an opportunity for understanding and empathy to flourish, helping to mend the wounds that separate us.

Empathy is a powerful tool in any relationship, and it plays a crucial role in healing emotional wounds and rebuilding fractured relationships. When we put ourselves in the shoes of our non-conservative children, we gain a deeper understanding of their experiences, struggles, and perspectives. This understanding cultivates a sense of compassion and fosters the foundation for reconciliation.

By taking the time to truly listen and understand their point of view, we validate their feelings and experiences. Empathy allows us to see beyond our own beliefs and biases, creating space for a genuine connection to form. It is through empathy that we can bridge the gap that separates us, finding common ground and building a bridge of understanding.

Empathy is not about agreeing with everything our non-conservative children say or do. It is about genuinely trying to understand their motivations and values, even if they differ from our own. It is about stepping outside of our comfort zones and allowing ourselves to embrace their perspective, no matter how challenging it may be.

When we approach our non-conservative children with empathy, we create an environment where they feel heard, seen, and valued. This can be a profound healing experience for them, as it helps to rebuild trust and restore the connection that was damaged by political disagreements. The power of empathy lies in its ability to transcend divisions and bring us closer together as a family.

In the process of healing wounds and rebuilding relationships, it is essential to make genuine efforts to reconnect with our non-conservative children. This requires a sincere and honest intention to bridge the gap that separates us and rebuild the trust that may have been shattered.

Making amends is an integral part of this process. Reflecting on our own actions and acknowledging any mistakes we may have made is a vital step towards healing. By sincerely apologizing for any hurt we may have caused, we demonstrate our commitment to growth and change. This act of humility opens the door to healing and lays the foundation for a healthier and more authentic relationship.

Furthermore, it is essential to show our non-conservative children that we have a genuine desire to reconnect. This may involve reaching out to them, expressing our desire to rebuild the relationship, and actively seeking opportunities for open and honest dialogue. By doing so, we communicate that their presence and well-being are important to us, and we are committed to working towards restoration.

Rebuilding relationships takes time and effort. It requires us to be patient and understanding, as healing cannot occur overnight. But if we approach the process with sincerity and a genuine desire to reconnect, we lay the groundwork for a new foundation, one built on understanding, respect, and love.

Communication is a powerful tool in the process of healing wounds and rebuilding relationships. It is through open and honest communication that we can address the issues that have caused the divide between us and our non-conservative children. It allows us to express our emotions, thoughts, and concerns in a healthy and productive manner.

To effectively communicate, it is crucial to practice active listening. Active listening involves not only hearing the words being spoken but also understanding the underlying emotions and intentions behind them. By actively listening to our non-conservative children, we create a sense of trust and validation, as they feel heard and respected.

Active listening requires us to be fully present in the conversation, free from distractions or judgment. It involves paraphrasing their words to ensure that we understand them correctly, asking open-ended questions to encourage further exploration of their thoughts and feelings, and reflecting their emotions to demonstrate empathy.

When we engage in active listening, we create a safe and respectful space for dialogue. This fosters a sense of trust and openness, allowing both parties to express themselves honestly and authentically. Through active listening, we can bridge the gap between us and our non-conservative children, replacing conflict with understanding and fostering a stronger, more resilient relationship.

In the process of healing wounds and rebuilding relationships, it is essential to redefine boundaries to establish healthy and respectful relationships. Boundaries serve as guidelines that protect the well-being and values of all parties involved while still allowing for mutual respect and understanding.

Redefining boundaries involves setting clear expectations for behavior and communication while also being open to compromise. It requires us to communicate our needs and boundaries assertively, ensuring that our non-conservative children understand and respect them. At the same time, we must be willing to listen to their needs and boundaries, finding common ground and seeking compromise when necessary.

Boundaries are not about control or exerting power. Instead, they are about creating a sense of safety and respect within the relationship. By clearly defining boundaries, we provide a framework for healthy interactions and mutual understanding. This fosters an environment where both parties can feel heard, respected, and valued.

Establishing boundaries also involves understanding and respecting the boundaries set by our non-conservative children. It is important to validate their experiences and perspectives, even if they differ from our own. By doing so, we demonstrate our commitment to a balanced and equitable relationship, fostering a sense of fairness and harmony.

Through the redefinition of boundaries, we create an environment conducive to healing and growth. It allows us to establish a solid foundation for healthy and respectful relationships, where both parties feel empowered and valued.

Trust is a fundamental element in any relationship, and rebuilding it is crucial in the healing process. Trust provides a solid foundation for open communication, vulnerability, and understanding. Without trust, it is challenging to forge a meaningful connection with our non-conservative children.

Cultivating trust involves consistency, reliability, and accountability. It means showing up when we say we will, following through on our commitments, and being accountable for our actions. Trust is built over time through a series of consistent and reliable interactions. It requires us to be dependable and to prioritize the needs and well-being of our non-conservative children.

To rebuild trust, we must also acknowledge and address any past actions or behaviors that may have caused harm or contributed to the fracture in the relationship. This requires taking responsibility for our mistakes and making amends where necessary. By demonstrating genuine remorse and a commitment to change, we show our non-conservative children that we are invested in rebuilding the relationship and restoring trust.

Rebuilding trust takes time and patience. It requires us to consistently show up, be reliable, and demonstrate our willingness to learn and grow. It also involves understanding and acknowledging the impact of past actions on our non-conservative children. Through consistent actions, reliability, and accountability, we can slowly rebuild the bridges that were broken, fostering a sense of trust, and deepening the connection between us.

In the process of healing wounds and rebuilding relationships, it is essential to engage in self-reflection and personal growth. Self-reflection involves looking inward and examining our own contributions to the fractured relationship, while personal growth involves taking steps towards self-improvement and change.

Self-reflection allows us to gain a deeper understanding of our own beliefs, biases, and behavior patterns. It requires us to honestly assess how our actions may have contributed to the divide between us and our non-conservative children. By acknowledging our own shortcomings and taking responsibility for our actions, we create space for growth and change.

Personal growth involves actively working towards self-improvement. It means challenging our own beliefs and assumptions, seeking to broaden our perspectives and actively engaging in self-education. Personal growth also involves practicing empathy, compassion, and emotional intelligence, as these qualities contribute to the development of healthier relationships.

Through self-reflection and personal growth, we become more self-aware and better equipped to mend the wounds that separate us from our non-conservative children. As we learn and grow, we are able to approach the healing process with greater compassion and understanding. Self-reflection and personal growth allow us to break free from old patterns of behavior and create a better version of ourselves, one that is more open-minded, understanding, and empathetic.

In the journey of healing wounds and rebuilding relationships, it is crucial to let go of the past in order to move forward. Holding onto past grievances and resentments only serves to perpetuate the cycle of pain and hinder the healing process. By choosing to let go, we release the emotional baggage that weighs us down and open ourselves up to the possibility of building a better and more fulfilling relationship with our non-conservative children.

Letting go is not about forgetting or condoning past hurtful actions. It is about acknowledging the pain and choosing not to let it define our future. It is about recognizing that we have the power to create a new narrative, one that is built on understanding, forgiveness, and growth. When we let go of the past, we embrace the present moment and focus on building a brighter future.

By letting go, we also free ourselves from the burden of anger and resentment. This emotional release allows space for healing and growth, both individually and within the relationship. We become more open to forgiveness, understanding, and empathy, and we create an environment where love and connection can flourish.

Letting go is a conscious choice, one that requires strength and courage. It is not always easy, but it is necessary for the healing process to begin. By letting go of the past, we create space for new beginnings and lay the groundwork for a more authentic and fulfilling relationship with our non-conservative children.

While the healing process can be undertaken independently, there may come a time when seeking professional help is necessary and beneficial. Trained professionals, such as therapists or counselors, can provide guidance, support, and an objective perspective that can aid in healing wounds and rebuilding relationships.

Professional help can provide a safe and non-judgmental space where both the conservative parents and their non-conservative children can explore their feelings, experiences, and perspectives. Therapists or counselors can facilitate productive conversations, help navigate difficult emotions, and offer strategies for rebuilding trust and reconciling differences.

Seeking professional help does not indicate a failure or weakness; instead, it demonstrates a commitment to growth and a willingness to invest in the relationship. Trained professionals can offer valuable insights and tools that can accelerate the healing process and provide a roadmap for a healthier and more fulfilling relationship.

In considering professional help, it is important to ensure that the therapist or counselor is experienced in dealing with family dynamics and political differences. Finding the right professional may take time, but the benefits of seeking their guidance can be tremendous in facilitating the healing process and rebuilding relationships.

In the journey of healing wounds and rebuilding relationships, it is essential to celebrate progress and small victories along the way. Healing takes time, and it is important to acknowledge and appreciate the efforts made by both ourselves and our non-conservative children.

By celebrating progress, we deepen the sense of connection and motivate further growth. It can be as simple as acknowledging and appreciating moments of genuine understanding, peaceful conversations, or shared moments of laughter. These small victories serve as reminders that healing is possible and that positive change is occurring.

Celebrating progress also reinforces the importance of perseverance and commitment. It reminds us that healing

Chapter 4: Cultivating Empathy and Understanding

The Empathy Deficit

Empathy is a fundamental aspect of human connection and understanding. It is the ability to put oneself in another person's shoes, to feel their emotions and experiences as if they were our own. In parenting, empathy is crucial for building a strong and nurturing relationship with our children. It allows us to truly understand their needs, emotions, and perspectives, fostering a sense of trust and support.

However, in conservative parenting, there can sometimes be a potential lack of empathy. This lack of empathy can significantly impact the parent-child relationship, leading to communication breakdowns, emotional disconnection, and ultimately, strained relationships. In this segment, we will delve deep into the empathy deficit in conservative parenting, exploring the contributing factors, consequences, and strategies for overcoming this deficit.

To fully understand the empathy deficit, we must first define empathy itself. Empathy involves the ability to recognize and understand the feelings of another person, acknowledging their experiences and validating their emotions without judgment. It is harnessing the power of emotional intelligence to connect with others on a deeper level. It is not simply feeling sorry for someone or sympathizing with their situation; it is truly understanding their thoughts, emotions, and perspectives.

In the realm of parenting, empathy plays a central role in creating a harmonious and loving bond between parent and child. It allows us to attune to our children's needs, respond to their emotions with sensitivity, and provide them with the validation and support they require. Empathy is the foundation upon which trust is built, ensuring that our children feel heard, understood, and valued.

However, in some cases of conservative parenting, empathy can be overshadowed by other beliefs and practices. Stricter disciplinary approaches and an emphasis on individual responsibility can inadvertently contribute to a potential empathy deficit. The focus on obedience and adherence to rules may leave little room for open dialogue and understanding. The urgency to teach personal responsibility can sometimes overshadow the importance of empathetic listening and emotional validation.

The consequences of this empathy deficit can be far-reaching and profound. Without empathy, children may feel unheard, silenced, or misunderstood within the family dynamic. When their emotions and experiences are not acknowledged or validated, they may struggle to develop a strong sense of self and trust in their own feelings. This can lead to emotional distancing and a breakdown in communication between parent and child.

Imagine a scenario where a conservative parent, focused on maintaining rule and order, dismisses their child's emotions as trivial or overdramatic. The child may internalize the message that their feelings are not valid or important. Over time, they may become reluctant to share their emotions, fearing judgment or rejection. This emotional disconnection not only strains the parent-child relationship but also inhibits the child's emotional growth and self-expression.

Generational and societal changes have further contributed to this empathy deficit in conservative parenting. With the rise of technology and changing societal norms, the opportunities for open and empathetic communication have transformed. Increased screen time and reliance on digital platforms have created barriers to authentic connections, making it more challenging for conservative parents to develop empathetic parenting skills.

Addressing the empathy deficit requires a shift in perspective and a willingness to challenge long-held beliefs. Parents must prioritize emotional validation, actively listening to their children without judgment or dismissal. They can cultivate empathy by modeling it themselves, respecting diverse perspectives, and exposing their children to a variety of experiences and ideologies.

Seeking outside support, such as therapy or parenting classes, can be immensely beneficial for conservative parents who wish to cultivate empathy in their parenting. These resources can provide guidance, tools, and a safe space for self-reflection and growth. Breaking the cycle of the empathy deficit requires effort, dedication, and a commitment to building a healthy and empathetic parent-child relationship.

In the following chapters, we will explore practical strategies and techniques for nurturing empathy in both conservative parents and their children. We will challenge stereotypes and misconceptions, emphasizing that empathy is not exclusive to any particular political ideology. We will delve into the power of empathy in bridging political differences and building strong, meaningful relationships between conservative parents and their non-conservative children.

Through real-life case studies and personal stories, we will inspire and encourage conservative parents to reflect on their own biases and beliefs. We will address potential resistance to the concept of the empathy deficit, offering strategies for engaging in constructive dialogue and fostering an open-minded approach to different perspectives.

Together, we will explore the transformative power of empathy in nurturing healthy and fulfilling parent-child relationships, regardless of political beliefs. The journey towards empathy begins here, and it is a journey that will strengthen and deepen the bond between conservative parents and their children.

Developing Empathy Skills

INTRODUCTION TO THE importance of developing empathy skills and enhancing emotional intelligence in order to improve relationships with non-conservative children. Highlight the benefits of empathy in fostering understanding and connection.

In a world that often feels divided and polarized, developing empathy skills is crucial for conservatives seeking to bridge the gap between themselves and their non-conservative children. Empathy is the ability to understand and share the feelings of others, and it plays a vital role in fostering understanding, connection, and ultimately, a stronger parent-child relationship.

At its core, empathy requires emotional intelligence, the ability to recognize, understand, and manage our own emotions as well as recognize and respond to the emotions of others. By cultivating empathy skills, conservative parents can create a safe and supportive environment for their non-conservative children, where their feelings and experiences are acknowledged and respected.

Exploration of the different types of empathy, including cognitive empathy (understanding others' perspectives) and emotional empathy (feeling others' emotions). Emphasize the importance of both types in building empathy skills.

Empathy can manifest in different forms, and understanding these variations is essential in developing empathy skills. Cognitive empathy refers to the ability to understand and appreciate others' perspectives, putting oneself in their shoes. Emotional empathy, on the other hand, involves feeling and sharing others' emotions, allowing us to connect deeply with their experiences.

Both cognitive and emotional empathy are necessary for building empathy skills. Cognitive empathy helps us develop a broader understanding of our non-conservative children's viewpoints, while emotional empathy allows us to connect with the emotions they may be experiencing. By developing both types of empathy, conservative parents can gain a more comprehensive understanding of their children's thoughts, feelings, and values, fostering empathy and building bridges of understanding.

Practical exercises for developing cognitive empathy, such as putting oneself in others' shoes and considering their experiences and perspectives. Provide specific examples and scenarios to guide readers in practicing cognitive empathy.

Developing cognitive empathy requires a conscious effort to understand others' perspectives, especially those that differ from our own. One practical exercise is to imagine ourselves in our non-conservative children's shoes, considering their experiences, values, and emotions. For example, we can ask ourselves how we would feel if our beliefs were constantly questioned or invalidated.

Another exercise involves actively seeking out diverse perspectives through reading books, watching documentaries, or engaging in conversations with individuals who have different backgrounds and ideologies. By immersing ourselves in these experiences, we can broaden our understanding and develop a more empathetic outlook.

Techniques for enhancing emotional empathy, including active listening and paying attention to non-verbal cues. Explain how these practices can help readers better understand and connect with their non-conservative children.

Enhancing emotional empathy requires active listening and attunement to non-verbal cues. When engaging in conversations with our non-conservative children, we can practice active listening by fully focusing on what they are saying, validating their emotions, and reflecting back what we hear. This conveys a sense of care and understanding, deepening the emotional connection between parent and child.

Paying attention to non-verbal cues, such as body language and tone of voice, is equally important. These cues can provide valuable insights into our children's emotions, helping us better understand their experience and respond with empathy.

Introduction to mindfulness as a tool for developing empathy skills. Discuss the benefits of mindfulness in increasing self-awareness and empathy towards others.

Mindfulness is a powerful tool that can help conservative parents develop greater self-awareness and enhance empathy towards others, including their non-conservative children. By practicing mindfulness, we become more present in the moment, allowing us to observe our thoughts, emotions, and reactions without judgment.

Through mindfulness, we can cultivate a deeper understanding of our own biases and beliefs, which is essential for developing empathy. Mindfulness allows us to detach from our automatic responses and open ourselves to new perspectives, ultimately fostering a more empathetic approach to parenting.

Guided meditation exercises for cultivating empathy and enhancing emotional intelligence. Provide step-by-step instructions for readers to follow along with the meditation practice.

One effective way to cultivate empathy and enhance emotional intelligence is through guided meditation practices. Here is a step-by-step meditation exercise for readers:

1. Find a quiet and comfortable space where you can sit or lie down without distractions.

2. Close your eyes and take a few deep breaths, allowing yourself to relax and center your attention.

3. Bring to mind a challenging situation involving your non-conservative child. Visualize the scene and the emotions that arise within you.

4. As you breathe, imagine sending compassion and understanding to yourself in that moment. Acknowledge any judgements or biases that may arise and let them go.

5. Now, shift your focus to your non-conservative child. Picture them in front of you, sensing their emotions and experiences.

6. As you breathe in, imagine embracing their emotions with compassion and understanding. Breathe out any resistance or judgment.

7. Repeat this process several times, focusing on sending compassion, understanding, and empathy to yourself and your non-conservative child.

8. When you feel ready, slowly open your eyes and take a few gentle breaths, bringing your attention back to the present moment.

In the following chapters, we will explore strategies and techniques for bridging the values gap between conservative parents and their non-conservative children. We will delve deeper into the power of empathy in navigating political differences and building strong, meaningful relationships.

Empathy skills will be key in this process, as they allow us to understand and appreciate our children's values and perspectives, even when they differ from our own. By further developing our empathy skills, we will gain insight into the underlying motivations behind their beliefs, fostering empathy and fostering constructive dialogue.

Together, we will explore the transformative power of empathy in nurturing healthy and fulfilling parent-child relationships, regardless of political beliefs. The journey towards empathy and bridging the values gap begins here, and it is a journey that will strengthen and deepen the bond between conservative parents and their non-conservative children.

Understanding Different Perspectives

THROUGHOUT OUR JOURNEY of understanding why our children won't talk to us, we have come to recognize the importance of empathy and understanding. In this segment, we will delve deeper into the concept of understanding different perspectives and explore how it can bridge the gap between conservative parents and their non-conservative children.

Empathy plays a pivotal role in fostering healthy parent-child relationships. As conservative parents, it can often be challenging to comprehend and accept our non-conservative children's perspectives. However, by cultivating empathy, we can begin to grasp their experiences and values on a deeper level. This understanding opens the door for meaningful communication and connection.

Stepping into our child's shoes is a vital step towards building empathy and understanding. By genuinely considering their experiences and perspectives, we can gain a deeper understanding of the challenges they face and the values that drive them. This practice not only enhances our ability to connect with them but also promotes improved communication and mutual respect.

Imagine for a moment the significant impact stepping into our child's shoes can have on our relationships. By placing ourselves in their position, we can better appreciate the adversity they may encounter or the struggles they face in expressing their beliefs. This deeper understanding allows us to respond in a more empathetic and supportive manner, ultimately strengthening the parent-child bond.

As conservative parents, we often hold certain assumptions about our non-conservative children that may hinder effective communication. These assumptions might revolve around their motivations, values, or the ideologies they align themselves with. It is essential to challenge these assumptions and open ourselves up to alternative perspectives.

By acknowledging and questioning our assumptions, we create space for meaningful dialogue and understanding.

Active listening is a powerful tool in understanding our non-conservative children's perspectives. When we truly engage in active listening, we give them the space to express themselves fully, without judgment or interruption. Techniques such as paraphrasing and reflecting back their thoughts and feelings demonstrate our commitment to understanding and validating their experiences.

By actively listening, we signal to our children that their voices are valued and respected, creating a safe environment for open and honest communication. For conservative parents who may find it challenging to navigate conversations with their non-conservative children, active listening is an invaluable skill that facilitates empathy and connection.

When engaging in conversations with our non-conservative children, it is crucial to approach them with curiosity rather than defensiveness. Curiosity allows us to genuinely inquire about their beliefs and experiences, genuinely seeking to understand rather than convince or impose our own views. By asking open-ended questions that invite dialogue, we create opportunities for mutual understanding and connection.

It can be transformative to explore shared experiences and find common ground during these conversations. For example, when discussing political or societal issues, we may discover that we share similar goals despite differing paths to achieving them. By focusing on these shared values, we can bridge the gap between differing perspectives and foster stronger relationships.

Validation is an essential aspect of empathy, even when we may not agree with our child's perspective. Validating their experiences means acknowledging and accepting their emotions and viewpoints, recognizing that their feelings are valid, regardless of our own beliefs. By doing so, we build trust and strengthen our parent-child relationships.

Even if we disagree with our child's opinions, it is crucial to separate validation from agreement. We can validate their experiences by expressing understanding, empathizing with their emotions, and acknowledging the challenges they face. This validation does not compromise our own beliefs but rather creates space for open and honest dialogue.

Finding shared values and principles can be a powerful means of bridging the gap between conservative parents and non-conservative children. When we identify these commonalities, we recognize that, at the core, we share fundamental aspirations for a just and prosperous society. By exploring these shared values together, we can create bridges of understanding and foster stronger connections.

Within our own families, it is essential to embrace diversity of thought. By doing so, we create an environment where different viewpoints are respected and valued. Encouraging respectful discussions and providing space for dissenting opinions fosters an atmosphere of understanding and growth.

By embracing diversity of thought, we can expose ourselves to new perspectives and ideas, challenging our own beliefs and promoting personal growth. This acceptance of differing viewpoints sends a powerful message to our non-conservative children—that we value their unique perspectives and are open to learning from them.

Self-reflection is a critical component of developing a deeper understanding of our non-conservative children's perspectives. It requires introspection, the ability to examine our own biases, and the willingness to challenge our preconceived notions. Through self-reflection, we can gain insights into our own motivations and biases, allowing us to approach conversations with greater empathy and understanding.

It can be helpful to engage in exercises that prompt self-reflection. For example, we can journal about our experiences, emotions, and beliefs, exploring how they may relate to our non-conservative children's experiences. Self-reflection allows us to cultivate greater self-awareness, which is essential for developing empathy towards others.

Communicating Empathetically

COMMUNICATION IS THE key to any successful relationship, and this holds true for the parent-child dynamic as well. When it comes to bridging the gap between conservative parents and their non-conservative children, it becomes imperative to communicate empathetically. By approaching conversations with understanding, respect, and an open mind, we create an environment where mutual growth and connection can thrive.

One of the first challenges we must face as conservative parents is understanding the communication hurdles that exist between ourselves and our non-conservative children. These hurdles stem from the fundamental differences in our beliefs, values, and perspectives. It is essential to acknowledge that these differences can lead to misunderstandings and conflicts, causing a disconnect between us and our children. By recognizing these challenges, we can begin to address them with empathy and find common ground.

Active listening and open-mindedness are powerful strategies for bridging the gap in communication. When we actively listen to our non-conservative children, we give them the space to express their thoughts and feelings fully. This means listening attentively, without interrupting or being dismissive. It also involves reflecting back their thoughts and feelings, showing that we understand and validate their experiences. Active listening fosters a sense of trust and respect, creating an environment where open and honest conversations can take place.

It is important for us as conservative parents to avoid judgment and criticism when engaging in conversations with our non-conservative children. While it is natural to have concerns and disagreements, expressing them through judgmental or critical language only serves to create a defensive and confrontational atmosphere. Instead, we should focus on expressing our concerns in a non-confrontational manner, using language that promotes understanding and empathy. This allows for a more productive and respectful dialogue.

Validating our non-conservative children's feelings and experiences is another crucial aspect of empathetic communication. Even if we may not fully understand or agree with their viewpoints, it is essential to acknowledge and empathize with their emotions. Validation does not mean we have to agree, but it does mean that we recognize and accept their emotions as valid. This validation builds trust and strengthens the bond between us and our children, fostering healthy relationships.

Finding common ground and shared interests can bridge the gap between conservative parents and non-conservative children. By focusing on topics or activities that both parties can relate to, we can create a sense of connection and understanding. This shared ground serves as a foundation for further conversations and builds bridges between differing perspectives.

The language we use in communication plays a significant role in fostering empathy and understanding. It is important to use neutral language that does not create a defensive or confrontational atmosphere. By choosing our words carefully, we can facilitate open and respectful dialogue. This means avoiding inflammatory or dismissive language and instead using words that promote empathy and understanding.

Non-verbal cues are also essential in communication. By paying attention to our non-conservative children's body language, facial expressions, and tone of voice, we can gain valuable insights into their emotions and experiences. These non-verbal cues allow us to respond with empathy and understanding, strengthening the connection between us and our children.

Patience and timing are crucial when engaging in conversations with our non-conservative children. It is important to choose the right moment to have these discussions, ensuring that both parties are receptive and open to understanding each other's perspectives. Pushing conversations at the wrong time can lead to further conflicts and hinder productive communication.

Utilizing reflective listening is a powerful tool in empathetic communication. By reflecting back our non-conservative children's thoughts and feelings, we show them that we genuinely understand and respect their perspectives. Reflective listening builds trust and establishes a sense of mutual respect, creating a conducive environment for open and honest conversations.

We must also encourage autonomy and embrace the differences in our non-conservative children's perspectives and choices. While we may have differing beliefs, it is important to support their individuality. By embracing their autonomy, we show them that we value their uniqueness and respect their choices. This fosters a sense of acceptance and strengthens our parent-child relationships.

Apologizing and repairing damages in communication is crucial when conflicts arise. As conservative parents, it is important for us to take responsibility for any hurtful or disrespectful comments we may have made. By apologizing sincerely and actively working to rebuild trust and connection, we demonstrate our commitment to a healthier and more empathetic communication dynamic.

Consistency in implementing empathetic communication strategies is key. It is important to apply these strategies consistently to build stronger relationships with our non-conservative children. This requires continuous learning and personal growth on our part, as we strive to improve our communication skills and broaden our understanding of their perspectives.

Communicating empathetically with our non-conservative children is essential for building healthier relationships. By focusing on active listening, open-mindedness, avoiding judgment and criticism, validating their feelings and experiences, seeking common ground, using neutral language, recognizing non-verbal cues, exercising patience and timing, utilizing reflective listening, encouraging autonomy and embracing differences, and apologizing and repairing when necessary, we can bridge the gap and establish a connection based on empathy and understanding. It is through these efforts that the parent-child bond can grow stronger, allowing for a more fulfilling relationship.

Support Systems and Community

ATTEMPTING TO BRIDGE ideological divides within families can be challenging to undertake alone. Support systems and community provide invaluable perspective, encouragement and accountability throughout this journey. By engaging with others, we gain strength and resilience.

Support groups allow us to share stories and strategies with like-minded parents and children seeking to heal family political rifts. The solidarity, empathy and practical wisdom offered can help us persist despite obstacles.

Religious or spiritual communities reinforce the principles of compassion and reconciliation when political tensions run high. Their teachings remind us to lead with love in turbulent times.

Professional organizations and nonprofits offer workshops, resources and mediation to assist families grappling with political differences. Their expertise lends structure and objectivity to the complex dynamics at play.

Therapy provides a neutral space to process emotions, gain self-awareness and develop communication tactics. Specialized family counselors can facilitate difficult conversations.

Friends and peers lend an empathetic ear when family relationships become strained. By confiding in trusted allies, we release the heavy burden of keeping struggles private.

Online forums enable us to virtually connect with a diverse community of people across geographic and ideological lines. This exposure to different viewpoints expands perspectives.

COACHING AND MENTORING programmes provide personalized guidance in applying reconciliation principles, maintaining motivation and progressing through obstacles.

Retreats and workshops focused on dialogue, empathy and reconciliation allow us to immerse ourselves in hands-on learning experiences to deepen understanding and reflection.

Interfaith coalitions harness the collective power of religious communities to find common ground on shared values like justice, compassion and human dignity.

Seeking community does not imply weakness or defeat - rather, it demonstrates wisdom, self-awareness and commitment to growth. By supplementing our own efforts with collective knowledge and mutual support, the path becomes more clear as we take each step forward in faith.

The Power of Validation

VALIDATION IS A POWERFUL tool in building and strengthening relationships, and it holds particular significance in the lives of non-conservative children. As conservative parents, it is crucial for us to understand that our children's experiences and emotions may differ from our own due to their unique perspectives and values. Disregarding or invalidating their feelings can have significant negative consequences, leading to strained relationships and a breakdown in communication.

Disagreements and conflict are natural in any relationship, and this holds true for the dynamic between conservative parents and non-conservative children. However, validation becomes even more important during these times. While our viewpoints may differ, it is essential to validate their experiences and emotions, even when we may not fully understand or agree with them. Validation involves actively listening and empathizing with them, acknowledging the validity of their emotions and experiences. By doing so, we open the doors to improved understanding and connection.

Practical examples of validation can be found in active listening and showing empathy. When our non-conservative children express their thoughts or feelings, it is crucial to give them our full attention and listen without interrupting or imposing our own viewpoints. Validating statements such as "I can see how that would make you feel that way" or "Your perspective is important to me" can go a long way in making them feel understood and accepted. This validation allows for healthier communication and a stronger parent-child bond.

It is understandable that as conservative parents, we may have concerns about validating differing viewpoints, fearing that it may be perceived as enabling or condoning behaviors or beliefs that go against our own values. However, it is crucial to recognize that validation does not mean agreement or condoning. Instead, it is about acknowledging the other person's perspective, allowing for respectful dialogue, and fostering open communication. By validating our non-conservative children's experiences and emotions, we create an environment where they feel heard and valued, leading to improved trust and relationship growth.

The benefits of validation are substantial. By validating our non-conservative children's experiences and emotions, we create a space for open and respectful dialogue. This improved communication opens opportunities for finding common ground and shared values, even with differing perspectives. The willingness to seek common ground and engage in open-minded conversations can lead to increased understanding, improved trust, and a stronger relationship between us and our children.

While practicing validation, it is important to maintain boundaries that ensure respect and healthy communication. Boundaries allow for individual autonomy while still acknowledging and accepting their emotions and experiences. By setting boundaries, we ensure that our non-conservative children's perspectives are respected, while also fostering an environment that encourages open dialogue and understanding.

Practicing validation requires implementing effective strategies. Reflective listening, where we actively listen and reflect back our non-conservative children's thoughts and feelings, shows them that we genuinely understand and respect their perspectives. Utilizing neutral language that avoids confrontation or defensiveness promotes empathy and understanding. Paying attention to non-verbal cues, such as body language and tone of voice, allows us to respond with empathy and better understand their emotions and experiences. Furthermore, choosing the right time and avoiding pushing conversations can facilitate open and productive communication.

Validation is an ongoing process. It requires continuous effort and personal growth on our part as conservative parents. We must consistently apply these strategies to build stronger relationships with our non-conservative children. This commitment to empathy and understanding not only bridges the gap but also allows for a more fulfilling and harmonious parent-child relationship.

The power of validation lies in its ability to foster empathy and understanding in our relationships with our non-conservative children. By actively listening, being open-minded, avoiding judgment and criticism, validating their feelings and experiences, seeking common ground, using neutral language, recognizing non-verbal cues, exercising patience and timing, utilizing reflective listening, encouraging autonomy and embracing differences, and apologizing and repairing when necessary, we can bridge the gap and establish a connection based on empathy and understanding. In doing so, we nurture and strengthen the parent-child bond, creating a more fulfilling and respectful relationship.

Chapter 5: Bridging the Values Gap

Exploring Core Values

Our core values are the very fabric of who we are as individuals. They go beyond mere preferences or opinions; they are the deeply held beliefs that shape our worldview and guide our decision-making. In the realm of family dynamics, understanding and acknowledging the core values of both conservative parents and their non-conservative children is crucial in bridging the seemingly insurmountable gap that often divides them. This chapter delves into the significance of exploring core values and how it can pave the way for constructive communication and reconnecting with our loved ones.

To truly explore core values, we must first define them. Core values are the principles and beliefs that we hold closest to our hearts. They are the unshakable truths that govern our perspectives and actions. Unlike mere preferences or opinions, core values are unwavering and play a central role in shaping who we are. By understanding this distinction, we can acknowledge the power and influence that core values have over our lives.

Conservative parents often hold deeply rooted core values that define their approach to life. These values are anchored in traditional family values, religious beliefs, and limited government intervention. For them, upholding the sanctity of the family unit, practicing their faith, and minimizing the interference of the state are of utmost importance. These core values greatly influence their parenting styles and political perspectives, offering a glimpse into their deeply held convictions.

On the other hand, non-conservative children tend to embrace core values that align with social justice, equality, and inclusivity. These values are often influenced by their educational experiences, exposure to diverse perspectives, and a resolute desire for change and progress. The younger generation sees the world through a lens that emphasizes fighting for equality, protecting the vulnerable, and challenging prevailing norms. Their core values manifest as a passion for shaping a more inclusive and equitable society.

The intersection of conservative parents' core values and those held by their non-conservative children can sometimes result in an undeniable clash. On issues such as LGBTQ+ rights, racial justice, or environmental sustainability, deeply entrenched beliefs pull in opposing directions. These clashes reverberate not only through passionate debates but also through strained relationships and emotional distress. Understanding the root cause of these conflicts requires exploring the very origins of our core values.

Core values do not simply materialize out of thin air. They are forged through a complex interplay of factors such as family upbringing, personal experiences, and societal influences. Conservative parents' core values may be shaped by their religious backgrounds, cultural heritage, and the historical context in which they grew up. Meanwhile, non-conservative children's core values may be grounded in their exposure to broader societal trends, evolving norms, and their generation's unique experiences. Recognizing these diverse origins can shed light on why core values diverge and why communication may falter.

Validation and respect are vital in any relationship, especially when it comes to acknowledging differing core values. Dismissing or belittling someone's deeply held beliefs not only fosters a toxic environment but also obstructs any potential for constructive dialogue. By validating and respecting each other's core values, even if they do not align, we open ourselves up to the possibility of understanding and growth. Both conservative parents and non-conservative children must recognize the profound impact of their words and actions on each other's emotional well-being and strive to foster an environment of acceptance.

When core values seem to diverge irreconcilably, it is essential to seek out common ground. Despite differing political orientations, conservative parents and non-conservative children are often united by shared values or aspirations. Whether it be the desire for a strong family bond, a safe and prosperous society, or the pursuit of personal happiness, uncovering these shared values can serve as a solid foundation for rebuilding and nurturing healthier relationships.

Building bridges necessitates open communication and active listening. Both parties must be willing to engage in respectful and empathetic dialogue. Reflecting on our own beliefs, asking open-ended questions to seek deeper understanding, and actively listening without judgment are crucial components of this process. By creating a safe space to express thoughts and emotions honestly, conservative parents and non-conservative children can begin to comprehend each other's core values more fully.

Empathy plays a pivotal role in bridging the gap between conservative parents and non-conservative children. It is through cultivating empathy that we can truly appreciate and understand the core values that shape the perspectives of those we love. Engaging in exercises and techniques that help develop empathy, such as role-playing, storytelling, or putting ourselves in each other's shoes, can deepen our understanding and pave the way for productive conversations.

In exploring core values, it is imperative to challenge assumptions and stereotypes that perpetuate division and polarization. Each individual is a complex and unique being, molded by their own experiences and beliefs. By letting go of preconceived notions about conservative parents or non-conservative children, we become more receptive to genuine connections. Viewing each other as individuals rather than subscribing to generalized narratives allows for authentic engagement and the potential for growth.

Sometimes, despite our best efforts, navigating the intricate dynamics of core values may seem overwhelming. In such cases, seeking support from professionals, such as therapists or family counselors, can provide a neutral space for constructive conversations. Impartial mediation can foster understanding, offer valuable insights, and help conservative parents and non-conservative children find common ground. Remember, seeking external assistance is not a sign of weakness; rather, it demonstrates a genuine commitment to improving familial relationships.

Understanding and exploring core values is a crucial step towards unraveling the mystery of why our children may be distant or unresponsive. By recognizing the significance that our core values hold in our lives and those of our children, we can start to bridge the gap and forge healthier connections. Only by embarking on this transformative journey can we hope to mend the strained ties and rediscover the love and understanding that lie beneath the surface.

Communicating Values Effectively

IN ORDER TO BRIDGE the gap between conservative parents and their non-conservative children, effective communication in values is of utmost importance. It is inevitable that discussions about values can lead to defensive reactions and conflicts, making it crucial for both parties to approach the topic with mindfulness and understanding. This chapter delves into strategies and techniques that can help conservatives communicate their values effectively, fostering a deeper connection with their children.

To effectively communicate values, conservative parents must make an effort to understand the perspectives of their non-conservative children. Active listening and empathy-building play a key role in this process. By truly listening to their children's viewpoints without judgment, parents can foster a deeper understanding of the values that guide their children's lives. It is through this empathetic understanding that meaningful conversations and connections can arise.

Accusations and judgments have a detrimental impact on communication, particularly when discussing values. Instead of attacking or criticizing opposing viewpoints, conservative parents can utilize techniques that allow them to express their values without pointing fingers. By focusing on the positive aspects of their values and explaining the reasons behind their beliefs in a calm and respectful manner, parents can create a non-confrontational environment.

An important aspect of effective communication in values is creating a safe and non-threatening environment for open conversations. Setting ground rules that prioritize respect, establishing a safe space where all opinions are welcomed, and maintaining decorum during discussions are essential strategies for fostering healthy dialogue. Building this environment will encourage children to freely express their thoughts and will enhance the chances of conservative parents being heard and understood.

Nonviolent communication techniques are invaluable tools in discussing values. By using "I" statements and expressing needs rather than making demands, conservative parents can maintain a non-confrontational approach that promotes understanding. For example, instead of saying "You should think this way," parents can say, "I feel strongly about this because it aligns with my personal values and I hope you can understand where I am coming from." This shift in language can create an atmosphere that encourages dialogue rather than defensiveness.

Discovering common ground and identifying shared values is crucial in bridging the gap between conservative parents and their non-conservative children. Despite differing beliefs on specific issues, there are often overarching values that both parties prioritize, such as love for family, the desire for a safe and prosperous society, or the pursuit of personal happiness. By finding and acknowledging these shared values, parents can foster a sense of connection and build upon those foundations.

Discussions about values can often evoke strong emotions in both conservative parents and their non-conservative children. It is essential to recognize and respond to these emotional triggers with calmness and respect. Remaining composed in the face of emotional reactions and actively listening to the underlying concerns can help de-escalate tense situations. By approaching these triggers with empathy and understanding, both parties can navigate conversations more effectively.

Effective communication of values involves active problem-solving and compromise. Recognizing that finding a mutually beneficial solution is more important than winning an argument or convincing the other party of one's viewpoint lays the groundwork for productive dialogue. Conservative parents can engage in discussions with the mindset of searching for common understanding and coming up with compromises that honor the values of both parties involved.

Nonverbal communication plays a significant role in reinforcing values. Conservative parents can utilize their body language, tone of voice, and other nonverbal cues to convey their dedication to their values and the importance they hold in their lives. Gestures of support, warmth, and encouragement can serve as powerful tools to reinforce the sincerity behind the discussions taking place.

Patience and persistence are essential qualities when it comes to effectively communicating values. Building understanding and connection takes time and effort. Conservative parents must remain committed to the process, even when faced with setbacks or resistance. By exercising patience and persistently working towards open and honest communication, parents can pave the way for stronger relationships with their non-conservative children.

An important aspect of effectively communicating values is celebrating differences and allowing for individuality. Conservative parents must recognize that their children's values may differ from their own and that these differences should be acknowledged and respected. Fostering an environment of acceptance and openness towards diverse perspectives is vital for healthy communication and relationship-building.

During conversations about values, it is crucial for conservative parents to provide support and encouragement to their non-conservative children. Validating their emotional experiences, even if their beliefs differ, and offering constructive feedback can foster an atmosphere of trust and understanding. By effectively supporting and encouraging their children, parents can strengthen the bond between them, paving the way for more fruitful conversations.

To improve communication, conservative parents must reflect on their own biases and assumptions regarding non-conservative values. Questioning preconceived notions and challenging ingrained beliefs is essential for deepening understanding and creating opportunities for growth. By consciously working to overcome personal biases and approach discussions with an open mind, parents can foster an environment of mutual respect and acceptance.

In order to make ongoing improvements in values communication, conservative parents must monitor their communication patterns. Regularly engaging in self-assessment, reflecting on past conversations, and identifying areas for growth can lead to more effective communication. By continuously examining their approaches and making necessary adjustments, parents can maintain an atmosphere of openness and understanding.

Actions and role modeling go hand in hand with effectively communicating values. Conservative parents should lead by example, aligning their behavior with their stated values. By embodying their beliefs and values in their actions, parents can convey the sincerity and depth of their convictions. Children often respond positively to consistent and authentic role models, amplifying the impact of values communication.

Seeking Shared Values

INTRODUCING THE CONCEPT of seeking shared values, I believe it is essential for conservative parents to actively seek common ground with their non-conservative children. This approach allows for a better understanding and connection, ultimately bridging the gap that may have formed over time. As conservative parents, we hold a significant role in initiating this process of seeking shared values and opening up a space for productive dialogue.

Exploring common ground is a crucial step towards rebuilding the relationship between conservative parents and their non-conservative children. Despite differing beliefs on specific issues, there are often overarching values that both parties prioritize. These shared values serve as a foundation for building understanding and connection. For example, both conservative parents and their children may value family, a safe and prosperous society, or the pursuit of personal happiness. By acknowledging and highlighting these shared values, we can find common ground and build upon it.

Of course, in seeking shared values, we must also navigate our differences respectfully. It is inevitable that conservative parents and their non-conservative children will have disagreements and differing opinions. However, it is essential to approach these conversations with an open mind and engage in respectful dialogue. By listening actively, valuing each other's perspectives, and finding common ground, we can explore our differences in a constructive manner.

Active listening plays a significant role in seeking shared values. By truly hearing our non-conservative children and understanding their perspectives, we can foster empathy and create a space for mutual understanding. As conservative parents, we must develop our listening skills, focusing on being present in conversations, avoiding interrupting, and demonstrating genuine interest in what our children have to say. Active listening allows us to bridge the gap between conservative values and the beliefs of our non-conservative children.

Finding the balance between compromise and staying true to one's values is crucial in seeking shared values. It is essential to remain authentic as conservative parents while also being open to compromise for the sake of fostering connection. This delicate balance allows for mutual respect and understanding while ensuring that conservative parents stay true to their beliefs. By finding common ground and exploring shared values, we can maintain our conservative principles while still connecting with our non-conservative children.

Addressing misunderstandings and stereotypes is an integral part of seeking shared values. As conservative parents, we must acknowledge the presence of misunderstandings and stereotypes that may have formed between us and our non-conservative children. These misunderstandings can hinder open dialogue and create barriers to connection. To overcome this challenge, we must actively debunk stereotypes and promote a culture of open dialogue, rooted in empathy and understanding.

Empathy plays a powerful role in fostering connection and understanding. Conservative parents must practice empathy by putting themselves in their children's shoes, seeking to understand their experiences and perspectives. Empathy allows us to bridge the gap between conservative values and our children's beliefs, forging a deeper connection based on shared emotions and a genuine desire to understand one another.

Mutual respect and validation are fundamental elements of seeking shared values. By valuing and respecting our non-conservative children's perspectives, we create an environment that fosters open communication. Validating their experiences, even if their beliefs differ, allows us to build trust and strengthens our bond. Mutual respect ensures that both parties feel heard and valued, facilitating the process of seeking shared values.

Taking small steps towards shared values is a practical approach to fostering understanding and connection. Conservative parents can initiate these steps by engaging in shared activities or exploring common interests with their non-conservative children. Starting with small changes and gradually building upon them allows the relationship to develop organically and encourages both parties to find common ground.

Celebrating differences and individuality is vital in seeking shared values. Conservative parents must recognize and respect that their children's values may differ from their own. By fostering an environment of acceptance and openness towards diverse perspectives, we create space for healthy discussions and relationship-building.

Throughout this journey, it is important to provide support and encouragement to our non-conservative children. Validating their emotional experiences, even when their beliefs differ, and offering constructive feedback demonstrates our commitment to their growth and well-being. By providing support and encouragement, we strengthen the bond between us and create an atmosphere of trust.

Reflecting on our own biases and assumptions is a necessary step in improving communication with our non-conservative children. We must question preconceived notions and challenge ingrained beliefs to deepen our understanding and create opportunities for growth. With an open mind and a commitment to personal growth, we can foster an environment of mutual respect and acceptance.

Monitoring communication patterns is crucial for ongoing improvement in values communication. Conservative parents must regularly engage in self-assessment, reflect on past conversations, and identify areas for growth. By continuously examining our approaches and making necessary adjustments, we create an atmosphere of openness, understanding, and connection.

Actions and role modeling go hand in hand with effectively communicating values. Conservative parents should lead by example, aligning their behavior with their stated values. By embodying our beliefs and values in our actions, we convey the sincerity and depth of our convictions. Children often respond positively to consistent and authentic role models, amplifying the impact of values communication.

To truly bridge the gap and build a stronger relationship with our non-conservative children, we must actively seek shared values. By practicing nonviolent communication techniques, finding common ground, embracing differences, and fostering empathy, we can create a foundation for understanding and connection. Throughout this process, we should celebrate the small victories, learn from our challenges, and continue to strive for better communication. Taking action and actively seeking shared values with our children is not only a personal journey but a necessary step towards a more cohesive and united family.

Embracing Differences and Diversity

TRADITIONAL THINKING, deeply rooted in conservative circles, often involves a rigid adherence to age-old beliefs and practices. While these beliefs may hold meaning and significance for us, they can also create barriers in our relationships, hindering understanding and acceptance. It is crucial for us to reflect on whether our traditional thinking may be causing strain in our relationship with our non-conservative children. By recognizing the limitations of our own conservative mindset, we can begin to open ourselves up to a broader understanding of the world and embrace the diversity of perspectives that surround us.

A key aspect of embracing differences and diversity lies in challenging our preconceived notions and biases. Within conservative circles, a range of biases may exist that prevent us from fully understanding and connecting with our non-conservative children. These biases can manifest in subtle ways, shaping our thoughts and actions. It is essential that we examine our own biases and actively work towards unlearning them. By doing so, we create space for growth and foster an environment that respects and values diverse perspectives.

Meaningful dialogue serves as the cornerstone of acceptance and inclusivity. Engaging in open and respectful conversations with our non-conservative children allows us to truly understand their perspectives and experiences. Active listening, avoiding judgment, and expressing our own thoughts and feelings in a non-confrontational manner are all key components of effective communication. Even when disagreements arise, it is vital that we maintain a respectful tone, demonstrating our commitment to understanding rather than imposing our own views.

Embracing differences and finding common ground are not mutually exclusive. It is possible to celebrate the diversity of perspectives while also seeking shared values. As conservative parents, we must learn to appreciate the uniqueness of our non-conservative children and recognize the value they bring to our lives. By embracing these differences, we create an environment of acceptance and foster a sense of unity that transcends conflicting values.

Building an environment of respect and inclusivity within our families requires conscious effort and a commitment to setting ground rules for communication and behavior. By establishing expectations that encourage acceptance and mutual understanding, we provide a safe space for our non-conservative children to express themselves freely. As conservative parents, we must lead by example, demonstrating through our actions and words the importance of respect and inclusivity in our family dynamics.

Stereotypes and misconceptions often cloud our understanding of our non-conservative children. Assumptions about their beliefs and values can hinder open communication and create distance between us. It is essential that we actively challenge and break down these stereotypes by approaching conversations with an open mind and genuine acceptance.

Education plays a critical role in fostering acceptance and understanding. By seeking out resources that broaden our understanding of diverse viewpoints, we can expand our horizons and engage in informed conversations with our non-conservative children. Books, films, documentaries, and other forms of media provide valuable insights into different perspectives, allowing us to engage in meaningful discussions and further develop our own understanding.

Empathy serves as a powerful bridge between conservative parents and their non-conservative children. By actively seeking to understand their experiences and perspectives, we can cultivate a deeper sense of empathy. This involves putting ourselves in their shoes, setting aside our own preconceived notions and judgments, and genuinely seeking to comprehend their emotions and motivations. Nurturing empathy and understanding creates a solid foundation for building stronger relationships based on acceptance and compassion.

Embracing personal growth as conservative parents is crucial in fostering stronger relationships with our non-conservative children. It requires a willingness to reflect on our own beliefs and biases, challenging ourselves to grow and evolve. Self-reflection, therapy, mindfulness exercises, and journaling are just a few examples of practices that can help facilitate personal growth. By actively engaging in this process, we can create an environment that encourages mutual acceptance and growth.

Personal growth is not a one-sided journey. Non-conservative children also play a crucial role in nurturing their relationships with their conservative parents. By approaching the relationship with understanding and empathy, they can foster a sense of mutual respect while appreciating their parents' perspective. Engaging in respectful discussions, seeking therapy, or exploring personal growth opportunities can help non-conservative children nurture their own growth while building stronger connections with their conservative parents.

Supporting each other's individuality is a cornerstone of a healthy parent-child relationship. As conservative parents, it is vital that we acknowledge and respect our non-conservative children's right to hold their own beliefs and values. By encouraging their autonomy and celebrating their individuality, we create an environment that nurtures open dialogue and understanding based on acceptance rather than disapproval.

Maintaining a healthy and evolving relationship with our non-conservative children requires continuous learning and adaptation. Staying open-minded and receptive to new ideas, even when they challenge our own beliefs, is key to growth. Flexibility and adaptability enable us to navigate the challenges of embracing differences and diversity, ensuring that we can consistently communicate our values in a way that fosters connection and understanding.

As parents, your behavior and attitude serve as a powerful influence on your children's development. Modeling acceptance and inclusivity in our words and actions is instrumental in shaping the family dynamic. By consistently demonstrating a genuine acceptance of diversity, we create an environment where our non-conservative children feel safe, valued, and respected. This open-mindedness allows for healthy dialogue and a stronger connection between us.

Promoting respect and inclusivity should extend beyond the boundaries of our immediate family. As conservative parents, we have a responsibility to advocate for these values within wider conservative communities. By engaging in open dialogue, challenging prejudice, and promoting acceptance, we can contribute to creating a culture that embraces diversity and fosters stronger connections among all members of society.

Embracing differences and diversity is a multifaceted journey that requires commitment, empathy, and self-reflection. By actively seeking shared values, challenging biases, engaging in meaningful dialogue, and fostering an environment of respect and inclusivity, we can bridge the gap between conservative parents and their non-conservative children. This path towards connection and understanding is not without its challenges, but the rewards of a stronger, more united family are well worth the effort. By continuously learning, growing, and adapting, we can create a future in which our differences are celebrated and our connections are fortified, one conversation at a time.

Building a Values-Based Relationship

IN THE PURSUIT OF BUILDING a values-based relationship with our non-conservative children, we must first understand the importance of values in family relationships. Values serve as the core foundation of our beliefs, guiding our thoughts, actions, and decisions. As conservative parents, it is crucial to recognize that our values may differ from those of our children who hold more progressive or non-conservative beliefs. These differences can create tension and strain in our relationships, often resulting in communication breakdowns and emotional distance.

Acknowledging the impact of political differences is a pivotal step in understanding our non-conservative children's values. Political ideologies often shape personal values, and when our children hold differing political views, it can be challenging for us to reconcile our conservative beliefs with their more progressive stance. However, it is essential to approach political discussions with empathy and openness. By seeking to understand the underlying motivations and experiences that shape our children's beliefs, we can foster a more respectful and constructive dialogue.

In nurturing respectful communication, conservative parents must adopt strategies that promote active listening and create a safe space for open dialogue. This means genuinely listening to our children's perspectives without interrupting or immediately invalidating their beliefs. Rather than rushing to offer counterarguments or judgments, we must prioritize understanding their experiences and emotions. By fostering an environment of respect and empathy, we create a foundation for effective communication that transcends the divide between differing values.

Finding common ground becomes a crucial aspect of building a values-based relationship. While political differences may seem insurmountable, it is essential to focus on shared goals and aspirations. By shifting our attention away from the political realm and toward common values such as love, compassion, and personal growth, we can discover areas of overlap that serve as bridges between our conservative values and their non-conservative beliefs. Compromise and collaboration allow both parties to feel heard and respected, paving the way for a stronger and more sustainable connection.

Boundaries and mutual respect are vital for maintaining a healthy values-based relationship. It is essential for conservative parents to acknowledge and respect their children's autonomy and growth. This means letting go of control and embracing their independence, even when it contradicts our own beliefs. By establishing boundaries that honor each individual's values and beliefs, we create an atmosphere of mutual respect that fosters trust and understanding.

Embracing personal growth and self-reflection is a transformative journey for conservative parents. By taking the time to reflect on our own values and beliefs, we can gain greater insight into the gap between our conservative worldview and our non-conservative children's perspectives. Personal growth allows us to challenge our biases, expand our understanding, and bridge the values gap with our children. Through this process, we open ourselves up to increased understanding and the potential for a stronger connection built on acceptance, compassion, and growth.

Practicing empathy and understanding is a powerful tool in nurturing a values-based relationship. By cultivating empathy towards our non-conservative children, we can gain a deeper appreciation for their lived experiences and the perspectives that shape their values. Seeing the world through their eyes allows us to connect on a more profound level and helps us navigate difficult conversations and conflicts with compassion and understanding.

Fostering compromise and collaboration is fundamental in bridging the values divide. It requires us to actively seek win-win solutions that honor both our conservative values and our children's non-conservative beliefs. By finding common ground and collaborating on shared goals, we can forge a path towards a stronger and more harmonious relationship.

Addressing difficult conversations and conflict is an inevitable part of navigating differing values. When these moments arise, it is crucial for conservative parents to approach them with an open mind and a willingness to understand. By actively listening, seeking common ground, and finding a middle ground, we can navigate conflicts in a constructive and respectful manner.

Celebrating individuality and diversity is key to embracing our non-conservative children's unique identities. As conservative parents, it is essential to appreciate and accept their right to hold their own beliefs and values. By creating a space that embraces diversity within our own families, we foster an environment of inclusivity and understanding, enriching our relationships and deepening our connections.

Ultimately, building a values-based relationship entails ongoing effort and communication. It requires a commitment to respect, compromise, and understanding. By continuously learning, adapting, and engaging in open and meaningful conversations, we can bridge the divide between conservative parents and their non-conservative children. Through these efforts, we pave the way for a future where our differences are celebrated and our connections are fortified, one conversation at a time.

Chapter 6: Rebuilding Trust and Connection

Understanding Trust Breakdown

Trust, a delicate thread that weaves the intricate fabric of a parent-child relationship, is a vital component in fostering love, understanding, and growth. However, within the complex dynamics between conservative parents and their non-conservative children, this trust is often strained, resulting in fractured connections and bewildered hearts. In this chapter, we delve into the depths of trust breakdown, unraveling the tangled web of emotions and experiences that contribute to the silence and distance between parent and child. Only by understanding the root causes of this breakdown can we hope to bridge the chasm and foster reconciliation.

Silence, the unseen wall that separates hearts, is often birthed from a lack of communication and openness. As conservative parents, we tend to hold steadfast to our beliefs and convictions, sometimes leaving little room for our children to voice their thoughts and emotions. The absence of open and honest dialogue stifles the growth of trust, hindering understanding and erecting barriers that can seem insurmountable. In this age of technological advancement, where communication is readily available at our fingertips, we must learn to embrace a culture of open conversation and active listening, creating spaces where each voice can be heard and validated.

Within the crucible of the parent-child relationship, divergent values and beliefs can ignite a fire that consumes trust. As conservative parents, we often cling to tradition and engrained ideologies, while our non-conservative children seek to challenge the status quo and chart their own paths. These fundamental disagreements can breed mistrust, as both parties struggle to comprehend and accept the stark differences in perspectives. To rebuild trust, we must acknowledge and honor the individuality of our children, valuing their autonomy and fostering an environment where mutual respect for differing beliefs is celebrated.

A rigid disposition, devoid of flexibility and an unwillingness to compromise, can be the bane of trust within parent-child relationships. Conservative parents, guided by deeply ingrained principles, can find it arduous to relinquish control or embrace alternative viewpoints. Conversely, non-conservative children, driven by their own convictions, often feel the need to challenge and change the world they inhabit. This clash of inflexible wills serves only to erode trust further. It is imperative that we practice the art of compromise, honoring the values we hold dear while demonstrating the willingness to navigate the gray areas of life. By doing so, we can cultivate an atmosphere of trust, where both parent and child can grow and evolve together.

Empathy, the bridge that spans the gap between hearts, often crumbles amidst the breakdown of trust. Empathy requires genuine understanding and a willingness to step into each other's shoes, yet as conservative parents, we may struggle to comprehend the passions and principles that fuel our non-conservative children. Conversely, these children may find it equally challenging to empathize with the life experiences and worldview of their conservative parents. Rebuilding trust necessitates developing empathy, fostering an environment where both parties seek to understand and validate each other's perspectives. It is through this empathic understanding that we can forge connections rooted in trust and harmony.

As conservative parents, we may inadvertently perpetuate trust breakdown through excessive criticism and judgment. Our desires to protect our children from the perceived dangers of the world can manifest as harsh criticism, stifling their growth and hindering trust. Similarly, non-conservative children may harbor resentment and feel judged for straying from the paths we have envisioned for them. A transformative paradigm shift is required, wherein constructive feedback replaces harsh judgment, and understanding replaces condemnation. By nurturing an environment of nonjudgmental support and encouragement, we can begin the process of repairing trust.

In some instances, trust breakdown within the parent-child relationship can be traced back to past instances of betrayal and breaches of trust. These scars run deep, leaving behind a trail of hurt and resentment that can linger for years. Healing and rebuilding trust requires a courageous journey of acknowledging and validating the pain caused, coupled with a commitment to forgiveness. The path is not easy, but if both parent and child are willing to confront the past and find solace in forgiveness, trust can be reborn, stronger and more resilient than before.

Trust breakdown is often intensified by unresolved conflicts and underlying resentment that lurks beneath the surface, poisoning the waters of connection. Conservative parents and non-conservative children may find themselves locked in a perpetual cycle of disagreement, unable to find resolution or closure. Yet, it is in facing these conflicts head-on, through honest and compassionate communication, that we can begin to heal the rift and rebuild trust. Deep-seated resentment must be acknowledged and addressed, making space for forgiveness and understanding to take root.

Within the context of parent-child relationships, trust can crumble due to a lack of boundaries and mutual respect. Boundaries provide a sense of safety and autonomy for both parties, allowing each to navigate the world with a sense of empowerment. As conservative parents, we may find it challenging to let go, leading to a disregard for the boundaries of our non-conservative children. Conversely, these children, seeking to assert their individuality, may disregard the boundaries we attempt to establish. Restoring trust requires establishing clear boundaries and fostering respect for each other's autonomy. Only through this mutual understanding can trust be rebuilt brick by brick.

The collision of divergent political beliefs, a hallmark of the strained dynamics between conservative parents and their non-conservative children, can have a profound impact on trust breakdown. Politics, often representing deeply ingrained values and ideologies, become the battleground where parent and child face off. The polarization and toxicity of the political landscape seep into the core of the parent-child relationship, leaving both parties wounded and distant. To rebuild trust, we must acknowledge the differing political perspectives, seeking to find common ground and understanding despite the ideological chasm that divides us.

Within the delicate tapestry of trust breakdown, emotional distance and withdrawal become tangled threads that pull parent and child further apart. The hurt, confusion, and frustration resulting from a lack of trust often breed emotional disconnect, causing both parties to retreat into their own emotional havens. To mend this rift, each must strive to find their way back to vulnerability, rediscovering the emotional connection that once flowed freely between them. The journey towards rebuilding trust necessitates embracing emotional vulnerability, allowing each heart to be seen and understood.

As conservative parents, we hold the power to initiate the healing and rebuilding of trust within our strained relationships with our non-conservative children. We must embark on a journey of self-reflection, examining our own biases, fears, and uncertainties. Understanding our role in the breakdown of trust is essential for progress. Through open and honest communication, empathy, and a commitment to understanding each other's perspectives, trust can be rekindled. Let us explore these strategies in the following pages, learning practical steps and exercises to foster trust and repair the strained connection between parent and child.

Rebuilding Trust Through Transparency

TRUST IS A FRAGILE entity, easily shattered but difficult to rebuild. In the intricate dance between conservative parents and their non-conservative children, trust breakdown often feels like a gaping void, tearing at the very fabric of the parent-child relationship. However, in this journey of healing and rebuilding trust, transparency holds the key to unlocking the doors of understanding and connection.

Transparency, in its essence, is the deliberate act of revealing oneself authentically, without fear or reservation. It requires a willingness to be seen, flaws and vulnerabilities bared, in the pursuit of truth and genuine connection. As conservative parents, we must recognize the power of transparency in restoring trust and embrace it wholeheartedly.

Transparency begins with self-awareness, a deep dive into our own beliefs, biases, and fears. By examining our own motivations and understanding the foundations of our conservative values, we can gain clarity and approach conversations with our non-conservative children from a place of authenticity. We must be willing to confront our own shortcomings and biases, acknowledging the ways in which our actions and beliefs may have contributed to the breakdown of trust.

Once we have embarked on this introspective journey, we can then extend an invitation to our non-conservative children to join us in the exploration of mutual understanding. Transparency in communication means creating a safe space for open dialogue, where both parent and child feel free to express themselves without judgment or condemnation. We must actively listen, not just to the words being spoken, but to the emotions and underlying concerns that lie beneath them. By truly hearing and validating the experiences and perspectives of our children, we can foster trust and create an atmosphere of acceptance.

But transparency goes beyond just communication; it permeates every aspect of our interactions with our non-conservative children. It involves being open and forthcoming about our own decision-making processes, sharing the rationale behind our beliefs and actions. Transparency allows our children to better understand our perspectives, even if they do not fully agree with them. It is in this act of sharing and inviting dialogue that trust can begin to take root.

Transparency also requires a commitment to consistency and reliability. Trust cannot be rebuilt if our words do not align with our actions. We must demonstrate our trustworthiness through follow-through and accountability, keeping our promises and commitments to our children. By showing up consistently and reliably, we send the message that we are committed to rebuilding trust and that our words hold weight.

In the realm of transparency, forgiveness plays a crucial role. We must be willing to acknowledge our own mistakes, apologize sincerely, and seek forgiveness from our children. Transparency means taking ownership of our actions and being brave enough to admit when we are wrong. Through this vulnerability, we pave the way for healing and rebuilding trust.

Rebuilding trust through transparency is a journey, one that requires patience, perseverance, and a commitment to growth. It is not a quick fix or a one-time action, but a continuous effort to bridge the gap between conservative parents and their non-conservative children. It is a dance of vulnerability, understanding, and mutual respect.

As we embark on this path towards rebuilding trust, let us lean into transparency with an open heart and an open mind. Let us be willing to confront our own biases, embrace vulnerability, and invite open dialogue. Through transparency, we can rebuild the trust that has been lost, creating a foundation for a stronger, more connected relationship with our non-conservative children.

Repairing Emotional Bonds

REPAIRING EMOTIONAL bonds between conservative parents and their non-conservative children requires a deep understanding of the emotional disconnect that often arises due to differing political beliefs and values. This disconnect can strain the parent-child relationship, creating a divide that seems insurmountable. However, it is crucial for parents to recognize and address this emotional disconnect in order to repair the bond with their children. It is a journey towards understanding and acceptance, where both parties need to be willing to explore and bridge the gap that has been created.

Repairing emotional bonds begins with open communication and active listening. It is imperative to create a safe and non-judgmental space where both parents and children can express their thoughts and feelings without fear of being dismissed or invalidated. Effective communication requires genuine curiosity and a willingness to understand each other's perspectives. Active listening plays a pivotal role in this process, allowing us to truly listen, reflect, and empathize with what our children are trying to convey. Through open communication and active listening, we can begin to rebuild the emotional bond that has been strained.

The power of empathy and understanding cannot be overstated when it comes to repairing emotional bonds. As conservative parents, we may find it challenging to understand our non-conservative children's viewpoints. However, by putting ourselves in their shoes and genuinely seeking to understand their experiences and beliefs, we can foster a deeper level of empathy. Cultivating empathy requires us to challenge our own biases and preconceived notions, embracing the idea that our children's perspectives are just as valid as our own. It is through empathy and understanding that we can bridge the divide and create a space for healing.

One crucial aspect of repairing emotional bonds is acknowledging and validating emotions. Dismissing or invalidating the emotions of both parents and children only further strains the relationship. Instead, we must make a conscious effort to validate our children's emotions, even if we may not fully agree with their beliefs. This validation does not mean we have to endorse their viewpoints, but it does require us to acknowledge the depth of their emotions and the validity of their experiences. Likewise, our non-conservative children must also validate our emotions, recognizing that our beliefs and values stem from our own lived experiences. By validating each other's emotions, we lay the groundwork for repairing the emotional bond.

Repairing emotional bonds involves finding common ground and emphasizing shared values. While political differences may seem irreconcilable, we can often discover common interests and hobbies that foster a renewed emotional connection. By identifying areas where both parents and children can connect, we create opportunities for open, respectful dialogue that transcends political beliefs. Shared values that bridge the gap can be as fundamental as love, respect, and the pursuit of a better future. Through the exploration of common ground and shared values, we uncover the unity that lies beneath our differences.

Sometimes, repairing emotional bonds requires the help of professionals. Seeking the guidance of therapists or counselors can provide invaluable support in facilitating conversations and navigating difficult discussions. These neutral third parties can provide insights and techniques that help both parents and children communicate more effectively and resolve conflicts. By involving professionals, we can approach the process of repairing our emotional bonds with a mediator's guidance, creating a safe space for open communication and shared growth.

Repairing emotional bonds is intricately linked with rebuilding trust and resolving past hurt. Trust issues and past conflicts can leave wounds that continue to strain the parent-child relationship. Resolving these conflicts involves addressing them with openness, honesty, and a willingness to find resolution. Patience and understanding become paramount as we work towards healing and rebuilding trust over time. We must confront the pain caused by past disagreements and find ways to move forward together, acknowledging that healing requires effort from both parents and children.

Setting boundaries and managing expectations are essential components in repairing emotional bonds. As conservative parents, it is crucial to communicate our personal boundaries and still maintain a loving and respectful connection with our non-conservative children. Likewise, our children must also respect our boundaries while expressing themselves freely. Clear communication is key, ensuring that both parties understand and accept each other's limits. By setting boundaries and managing expectations, we create a space that maintains mutual respect and fosters a healthy reconnection.

Cultivating forgiveness and letting go is a pivotal step in repairing emotional bonds. Holding onto past mistakes and resentment hinders the possibility of reconciliation and rebuilding trust. By cultivating forgiveness, we release the grip of negativity that can poison our relationships. It requires us to dig deep and find the strength within ourselves to let go of grudges, to accept apologies, and to move forward with genuine forgiveness. For both parents and children, practicing forgiveness creates the space necessary for healing and the emotional reconnection that follows.

Ultimately, repairing emotional bonds requires celebrating individuality and embracing differences. We must let go of the desire to change our non-conservative children and instead focus on accepting and appreciating their unique perspectives and experiences. By celebrating their individuality and embracing our differences, we create an environment where personal growth and development can flourish. We acknowledge that our children are their own individuals, entitled to their own beliefs and opinions. It is through acceptance and love that we build a foundation for a stronger, more connected relationship with our non-conservative children.

Repairing emotional bonds between conservative parents and their non-conservative children is no easy task. It requires patience, understanding, and a commitment to growth from both parties. This journey of love and reconciliation demands vulnerability, open-mindedness, and courageous self-reflection. But when we embark on this path, when we embrace transparency, rebuild trust, and celebrate our differences, we create the possibility of a renewed emotional bond, one that transcends political beliefs and fosters a deeper connection between parent and child. Through this journey, we can find common ground, bridge the divide, and heal the wounds that have strained our relationships. May love guide us as we embark on this path of repairing emotional bonds and reclaiming the connection with our non-conservative children.

Setting Boundaries and Self-care

IN THE PROCESS OF REBUILDING trust and emotional bonds, it's important not to overlook the importance of setting healthy boundaries and taking care of oneself. This is vital for both parents and children, irrespective of their ideological stances.

Setting healthy boundaries is not an act of separation or disconnect; rather, it's an essential step in preserving individual autonomy and emotional well-being. Boundaries are not walls; they're guidelines for how we want to be treated and what we expect from others. As conservative parents, understanding the importance of boundaries allows us to respect the individuality and autonomy of our non-conservative children. It enables us to have more balanced and respectful interactions, providing a framework within which a meaningful relationship can flourish.

For non-conservative children, setting boundaries is equally crucial. It provides them with the space they need to grow, explore, and become their own persons, separate from the familial expectations and ideologies that may be incongruent with their own beliefs.

Self-care goes hand in hand with setting boundaries. Emotional and mental well-being are foundational to any form of relationship. As conservative parents, we often put the needs of our family above our own, which can lead to burnout and resentment. It's important to recognize that taking time for ourselves is not selfish; rather, it's an act of self-preservation that benefits everyone around us. By being emotionally balanced and mentally rested, we can approach our relationships, including the one with our non-conservative children, from a place of love, understanding, and strength.

Likewise, our children must understand the value of self-care. The stresses and strains of navigating a complex relationship can take a toll on their well-being. It's important for them to take time for self-reflection, relaxation, and activities that bring them joy. In doing so, they recharge their emotional batteries and are better equipped to engage in meaningful dialogues and confront challenges.

To sum up, setting healthy boundaries and prioritizing self-care are essential elements in maintaining a balanced parent-child relationship. These practices can be the safety nets that prevent minor disagreements from escalating into significant emotional conflicts, thus offering a more nurturing environment for trust to be rebuilt and for emotional bonds to be strengthened.

Forgiveness and Letting Go

FORGIVENESS AND LETTING go are two essential components of reconciliation between conservative parents and their non-conservative children. In order to heal the wounds that have strained their relationship, both parties must embrace the power of forgiveness and the art of letting go. These practices are not easy, but they are vital for moving towards a healthier and more connected relationship. By exploring forgiveness and letting go, we open the door to healing past grievances and rebuilding the emotional bond that has been fractured.

Holding onto past grievances and resentments has a negative impact on both conservative parents and their non-conservative children. The weight of resentment hinders communication, understanding, and connection between family members. It acts as a barrier, preventing the vulnerable conversations necessary for reconciliation from taking place. Furthermore, the emotional toll of resentment can lead to increased stress, anxiety, and even physical health problems. In order to truly mend the parent-child relationship, both parties must recognize the detrimental impact of holding onto resentment.

While forgiveness may be challenging, the benefits it brings are undeniable. By choosing to forgive, individuals can experience a profound sense of liberation and emotional well-being. Forgiveness reduces stress and promotes a sense of inner peace, allowing parents and children to move forward without the weight of the past holding them back. Moreover, forgiveness enhances relationships, fostering a greater sense of connection, empathy, and understanding. Through forgiveness, both parents and non-conservative children can find healing and begin to rebuild their relationship on a foundation of love and acceptance.

Letting go of past hurts is a crucial step in the process of reconciliation. It requires conservative parents to practice empathy, shifting their perspective to understand their non-conservative children's experiences and beliefs. It also necessitates both parents and children to acknowledge and process the emotions associated with past grievances. This might involve seeking therapy or counseling to provide a safe space for this emotional exploration. Letting go does not mean forgetting or condoning past actions, but rather breaking free from the chains of resentment and creating the space for healing and growth.

In the journey towards repairing the parent-child relationship, it is essential for conservative parents to engage in self-reflection and take responsibility for any harm caused. This involves a willingness to examine their own actions, acknowledge the mistakes made, and offer themselves compassion and understanding. Through self-forgiveness and self-acceptance, parents can create a mindset that is open to growth and change. This self-awareness and humility pave the way for greater understanding and connection with their non-conservative children.

Building empathy and compassion is a vital component of the reconciliation process. Both parents and non-conservative children need to develop a deep understanding of each other's perspectives and experiences. This requires active listening, open-mindedness, and a readiness to step into the shoes of the other person. Exercises and techniques can be employed to cultivate empathy, such as engaging in active dialogue, reading books from different viewpoints, or seeking out diverse perspectives in the media. By committing to developing empathy and compassion, parents can bridge the gap and foster understanding with their non-conservative children.

It is not uncommon for conservative parents to face resistance when considering forgiveness. This resistance can stem from fear, pride, or a sense of self-righteousness. However, in order to repair the parent-child relationship, it is necessary to address and overcome these obstacles. This can be achieved through deep self-reflection, open communication with their non-conservative children, and a willingness to let go of old beliefs and preconceptions. By challenging their own resistance and embracing forgiveness, conservative parents create an opportunity for healing and the prospect of a renewed bond.

Forgiveness is not an end in itself but rather a means to an end - the ultimate goal of reconciliation between conservative parents and their non-conservative children. This reconciliation is founded on open dialogue, active listening, and mutual understanding. It involves parents showing genuine curiosity in their children's lives, beliefs, and experiences, while children reciprocate with respect and an openness to their parents' perspectives. Through forgiveness, parents and children can bridge the gap, find common ground, and work towards a more authentic and loving relationship.

Forgiveness is not a one-time event but rather a continuous process that requires effort and commitment. As conservative parents navigate their relationship with non-conservative children, they may encounter future conflicts or disagreements. In these moments, it is important to revisit the practice of forgiveness and letting go. By reminding themselves of the benefits forgiveness brings and actively choosing forgiveness in each new situation, parents can maintain the emotional connection with their children and continue on the journey of healing.

The power of forgiveness and letting go cannot be understated in the journey towards repairing the relationship between conservative parents and their non-conservative children. By embracing forgiveness, both parents and children create a space for healing, understanding, and connection. It is a process that demands vulnerability, open-mindedness, and courageous self-reflection. Yet, as conservative parents work towards letting go of past grievances, embracing empathy and compassion, and practicing forgiveness, they pave the way for growth and transformation. They celebrate the healing of their relationship and the deepening bond with their non-conservative children. In this celebration, both parents and children find hope for a future defined by love, acceptance, and a genuine appreciation for one another's unique experiences and perspectives.

Moving Forward With Mutual Respect

AFTER EXPLORING THE impact of political differences on family relationships and recognizing the importance of mutual respect, it is crucial for conservative parents to take the necessary steps to move forward with their non-conservative children. This requires a genuine effort to understand their children's perspectives and experiences, as well as a commitment to open and respectful communication.

To bridge the divide between conservative parents and non-conservative children, it is essential for parents to make an effort to understand their children's beliefs and experiences. This involves empathy and open-mindedness, as well as a willingness to challenge one's own preconceptions. By actively seeking to understand their children's viewpoints, conservative parents can create a foundation of understanding and growth.

Effective communication is key in navigating conversations about politics and other sensitive topics. Conservative parents and their non-conservative children must practice patience and kindness when discussing their differing beliefs. It is important to listen actively, without interrupting or dismissing the other person's point of view. By adopting a compassionate and understanding approach, both parents and children can foster healthy communication and maintain respect for each other.

Finding common ground between conservative parents and non-conservative children is essential for building bridges and fostering understanding. Shared activities or discussions that focus on shared values and interests can help to bridge the gap and create a sense of unity. By actively seeking out areas of agreement, conservative parents and their children can find common ground and strengthen their bond.

Accepting and appreciating each other's differences is vital in moving forward with mutual respect. Conservative parents should embrace their non-conservative children's individuality and allow them the freedom to explore their beliefs and values. Likewise, non-conservative children must also respect and appreciate their parents' conservative beliefs. By celebrating diversity within the family, both parents and children can create an environment that values individuality and promotes a sense of belonging.

Fostering a culture of learning and growth within the family is important for both conservative parents and non-conservative children. Engaging in informed discussions, encouraging critical thinking, and seeking out diverse perspectives can help to broaden everyone's understanding and promote respectful dialogue. By creating an environment that values learning and encourages intellectual curiosity, conservative parents and their children can continue to grow and evolve together.

Personal growth is a lifelong journey that requires self-reflection and a willingness to challenge one's own beliefs and values. Conservative parents should reflect on their own biases and consider alternative viewpoints. This commitment to personal growth allows for greater understanding and empathy towards their non-conservative children. By embracing personal growth, conservative parents can create a positive example for their children and foster stronger relationships based on mutual respect.

Healthy discussions about political differences can promote understanding and bridge the gap between conservative parents and non-conservative children. It is important to encourage respectful debate, where disagreement is welcomed but with a commitment to maintaining respect and open-mindedness. Setting guidelines for these discussions, such as avoiding personal attacks and focusing on the issues, can help facilitate productive conversations.

While understanding and respect are crucial, it is important for both conservative parents and non-conservative children to recognize their limitations in changing each other's beliefs. It is unrealistic to expect complete agreement, and setting boundaries allows for a healthy balance in the parent-child relationship. By respecting each other's boundaries and avoiding attempts to change or convert, both parents and children can navigate their differences in a respectful manner.

In some cases, conflicts in the parent-child relationship may require professional intervention. If attempts to repair the relationship independently have been unsuccessful, conservative parents and their non-conservative children should not hesitate to seek counseling or therapy. A trained professional can provide guidance, facilitate constructive dialogue, and help both parties navigate their differences in a healthy and productive manner.

Shared values and traditions can serve as a cornerstone for unity and understanding between conservative parents and non-conservative children. It is important to focus on the aspects that bring the family together rather than the differences that divide them. By celebrating shared values and traditions, both parents and children can foster a sense of belonging and unity within the family.

The process of forgiveness is essential in repairing the strained relationship between conservative parents and non-conservative children. This begins with acknowledging past grievances and taking steps to let go of anger and resentment. Forgiveness does not mean forgetting or condoning past actions, but rather freeing oneself from the burden of bitterness and creating a space for healing and growth.

Moving forward with mutual respect requires a commitment to continuous growth and understanding. Both conservative parents and non-conservative children must be willing to work on the relationship and maintain mutual respect. This entails ongoing self-reflection, open communication, and a willingness to embrace change. By committing to continuous growth, both parents and children can continue to strengthen their bond and foster a relationship grounded in respect and love.

Chapter 7: Embracing Personal Growth

The Power of Self-Reflection

Through self-reflection, you begin to recognize the influence of your own biases and preconceived notions. This awareness allows you to shine a light on hidden prejudices that color your interactions with your non-conservative children. You realize that these biases have been hindering your relationship, creating barriers instead of bridges. It becomes clear that if you truly want to reconnect with your children, confronting these biases head-on is essential.

Uncovering hidden beliefs is another profound revelation that self-reflection offers you. Through this introspective journey, you come face to face with deeply ingrained beliefs that have been influencing your interactions with your children for years. These beliefs shape your perspectives and reactions, often clouding your ability to empathize and understand their points of view. By examining these beliefs, you can dismantle their stronghold and develop a greater sense of empathy and understanding.

Perhaps the most transformative aspect of self-reflection is its ability to challenge the rigid ideologies that have been part of your conservative identity for so long. It enables you to step outside the confines of your own beliefs and embrace a more open-minded perspective. This newfound flexibility not only positively impacts your relationship with your children but also allows you to engage in meaningful dialogues with them, free from the constraints of dogma.

Through self-reflection, you begin to develop emotional intelligence—the ability to understand and manage emotions, both within yourself and in relation to others. This is a crucial element in bridging the gap between your conservative values and the differing beliefs of your children. It enables you to approach interactions with empathy and compassion, creating a safe space for open dialogue and mutual understanding.

By engaging in self-reflection, you can identify patterns of behavior and emotional triggers that have contributed to conflicts with your children. These insights offer an opportunity to recognize and address these patterns, leading to healthier and more productive interactions. Self-reflection becomes a tool for self-improvement, allowing you to break free from destructive cycles and create a more harmonious relationship with your children.

Challenging assumptions and stereotypes is another significant outcome of your journey of self-reflection. It encourages you to question preconceived notions you hold about your non-conservative children, opening your mind to the possibility of discovering their unique perspectives and experiences. This shift in mindset fosters curiosity and a genuine desire to understand, ultimately creating space for connection and acceptance.

Through the power of self-reflection, you cultivate a growth mindset—a belief in the capacity for personal growth and change. This mindset is essential in your journey to reconnect with your non-conservative children. It allows you to embrace new ideas, challenge your own beliefs, and adapt to the ever-evolving dynamics of your relationship. This mindset not only transforms your interactions but also fosters personal growth within you.

In your pursuit of understanding, self-reflection becomes a means of fostering self-acceptance. It teaches you to accept your own biases and beliefs as part of who you are, without judgment or guilt. This self-acceptance serves as an integral foundation for building stronger connections with your non-conservative children. By embracing your own imperfections and biases, you foster an environment that encourages openness and authenticity.

Applying self-reflection to everyday interactions becomes a habit that transforms your relationship with your children. You learn to pause and reflect before reacting, to consider their perspectives, and to respond with empathy and understanding. Small, consistent efforts bring about significant changes, creating a safe space for dialogue and fostering a sense of mutual respect.

While self-reflection is a deeply personal journey, seeking external support can be invaluable. Therapy or coaching can provide guidance and perspective from a neutral source, enabling you to navigate your journey of self-reflection with greater ease. These resources offer tools and strategies that can facilitate personal growth and enhance the quality of your parent-child relationship.

Remember, self-reflection is an ongoing practice, not a one-time task. It requires commitment, openness, and a willingness to continuously learn and evolve. By engaging in regular self-reflection, you can nurture and strengthen your relationships with your non-conservative children, creating a space where love, understanding, and acceptance can thrive.

The power of self-reflection cannot be underestimated. It is a transformative tool that allows you to understand your biases, uncover unconscious beliefs, challenge rigid ideologies, and develop emotional intelligence. Through self-reflection, you can identify patterns, challenge assumptions, cultivate a growth mindset, foster self-acceptance, and apply these learnings to everyday interactions. It is through this ongoing practice that you can reconnect with your non-conservative children, fostering stronger and more meaningful relationships.

Challenging Assumptions and Stereotypes

AS YOU VENTURE INTO the realm of questioning assumptions and stereotypes, you'll begin to grasp the power that lies in scrutinizing long-held narratives about non-conservative individuals. Understand that assumptions aren't just idle thoughts; they are the lenses through which you perceive and interact with others. These assumptions can either build bridges or create barriers in forging meaningful connections.

Stereotypes often stem from these assumptions. They are the broad generalizations and oversimplifications attributed to groups based on limited information. If you're a conservative parent, you may unwittingly cling to stereotypes about non-conservative individuals, which can taint your perception and impede open communication with your children.

To break free from these limiting beliefs, it's crucial to scrutinize your own values and ask why they shape your assumptions and stereotypes. This introspection calls for honesty and vulnerability as you confront the biases that have skewed your perspectives. It won't be easy; it means challenging long-established beliefs and facing uncomfortable truths about yourself.

On this introspective journey, you'll find that curiosity and open-mindedness are indispensable tools for challenging assumptions. Cultivating a genuine interest in understanding others enables you to move beyond surface-level differences and engage in deeper conversations. This requires setting aside preconceived notions and seeking out diverse perspectives.

Be aware of confirmation bias, the tendency to favor information that confirms your existing beliefs while ignoring evidence to the contrary. Recognizing this bias is a critical step toward dismantling stereotypes, requiring you to consciously seek out perspectives that challenge your existing worldview.

Empathy becomes a crucial guide on this journey. By putting yourself in the shoes of your non-conservative children, you can better understand the emotions, values, and experiences that shape their viewpoints. This calls for actively listening to their stories, acknowledging their lived experiences, and giving them a platform to express themselves.

Questioning preconceived notions becomes a liberating endeavor. It frees you from rigid ideologies and opens up new avenues for understanding. By shedding assumptions and embracing nuance, you can appreciate the richness that comes from understanding a diverse array of beliefs and identities.

Unlearning stereotypes is a gradual process demanding self-reflection and conscious effort. It involves challenging ingrained narratives and seeking counterexamples that debunk narrow generalizations. This journey calls for continuous self-reflection, humility, and a willingness to evolve.

Creating dialogue becomes the cornerstone of efforts to dismantle assumptions and stereotypes. Meaningful conversations are less about converting others to your views and more about building bridges based on understanding, empathy, and mutual respect. It requires valuing relationships above ideological differences and committing to open communication.

Throughout this process, learn to appreciate the complexity of individual beliefs and identities. No single "non-conservative" perspective exists; people's viewpoints are shaped by their unique experiences, values, and aspirations. By embracing this complexity, you deepen your appreciation for the rich tapestry of ideas in the world.

Challenging assumptions and stereotypes can be unsettling and even frightening. Stepping out of your comfort zone is an inherent part of growth. Seek support from like-minded individuals or communities navigating similar challenges; their shared experiences and wisdom can offer comfort and guidance.

This journey is an ongoing process that requires patience, resilience, and a commitment to self-reflection. Setbacks and frustrations may occur, but each step forward brings you closer to a deeper understanding of both yourself and your non-conservative children.

To continue this dialogue, resources like books, podcasts, and workshops can offer further exploration and insights. Cultivate a mindset of lifelong learning by engaging with open-minded individuals to enhance your understanding and empathy towards those who hold different beliefs.

Challenging assumptions and stereotypes is a commitment to self-reflection, empathy, and open-mindedness. By examining your assumptions, questioning preconceived notions, and actively seeking diverse perspectives, you can foster deeper understanding and stronger connections with those who think differently. This journey may be ongoing, but it holds the promise of creating spaces where love, acceptance, and understanding can thrive.

Seeking Knowledge and Education

ENGAGING WITH KNOWLEDGE and education can be a transformative journey for conservative parents. This path opens eyes to new perspectives, challenges worldviews, and expands understanding of non-conservative individuals. The value and importance of knowledge in broadening one's horizons and fostering mutual understanding can't be overstated.

Education serves as a pivotal channel for developing empathy. Through it, individuals gain the skills to understand and relate to different experiences and viewpoints. Exposure to a variety of perspectives via education enables better communication with non-conservative children, allowing an understanding of the emotions, values, and experiences that inform their perspectives.

There are numerous avenues for learning that can be crucial in this journey. From books and documentaries to online courses and workshops, a wide array of resources can help people broaden their understanding and engage in meaningful conversations with individuals who hold differing viewpoints. Utilizing these resources is essential for gaining a comprehensive understanding of others' perspectives.

Fostering intellectual curiosity is a key part of embracing education's full benefits. By nurturing your own curiosity and encouraging the same in young individuals with different viewpoints, a culture of lifelong learning and personal growth is promoted. Such curiosity allows for the engagement with new ideas, challenges to personal beliefs, and the continual expansion of understanding.

Constructive dialogue is essential for building stronger relationships. It demands active listening, open-mindedness, and a willingness to learn from different perspectives. Discussions that are respectful and emphasize mutual understanding create an environment conducive to meaningful conversation, bridging potential divides.

Education can also establish a common ground for people to connect over shared interests. Actively looking for opportunities to learn together can strengthen interpersonal bonds and show a commitment to understanding and relating to each other.

It's important to recognize and challenge any misconceptions and stereotypes that may exist. Education serves as a tool to break down these barriers, encouraging the questioning of preconceived notions and the active seeking of alternative viewpoints. By embracing education, you promote greater understanding and acceptance.

Adoption of a growth mindset is crucial. A focus on continuous learning and personal development can improve relationships and make discussions and disagreements more productive. With a growth mindset, conversations are approached with an open mind and a willingness to learn, enhancing interpersonal connections.

Critical thinking is another vital skill, important for evaluating information and for having informed discussions. By enhancing your critical thinking abilities and encouraging the same in others, you equip yourselves with the tools needed to discuss potentially sensitive or controversial topics. Empathy, respect, and a focus on common ground are key in these interactions.

Community involvement in education initiatives is also important for fostering connection and understanding. Active participation in local educational opportunities and advocating for equal opportunities for all not only strengthens community bonds but can also enhance relationships with those who hold different views.

Seeing education as a lifelong journey is vital for fostering greater understanding and connection. By continuously seeking knowledge, promoting intellectual curiosity, and embracing growth, you show a commitment to personal development, which can only enhance relationships with those of differing beliefs.

Respectful engagement with non-conservative perspectives is crucial. Actively listening, asking thoughtful questions, and aiming to understand different viewpoints without judgment opens up new avenues for understanding and collaboration.

The transformative impact of education on familial and social dynamics can't be ignored. It has the potential to improve relationships, increase understanding, and create stronger bonds between those of differing perspectives. It can also be instrumental in shaping individual identities and worldviews, thereby bridging gaps and fostering connection.

The pursuit of knowledge and education can be a journey of personal growth and transformation. It allows for the challenging of assumptions, the shedding of stereotypes, and the welcoming of new perspectives. Through the embrace of education, empathy cultivation, and constructive dialogue, stronger, more understanding relationships can be built. This journey calls for ongoing self-reflection, resilience, and a commitment to lifelong learning. Together, the gap can be bridged, leading to greater love, acceptance, and harmony in relationships with those who hold differing views.

Accepting What You Can't Change

AS CONSERVATIVE PARENTS trying to connect with your non-conservative children, it is important to recognize your limitations. There are certain things you simply cannot change, no matter how much you may wish to. Accepting these realities frees you to focus your energy where it can make a difference - on yourselves.

You cannot change your adult children's core values and political beliefs. Their perspectives have been shaped over time by many influences beyond our control. Pressuring or shaming them to conform to your views will only strain your relationship.

While you can share your beliefs and experiences, you cannot control how your children interpret or internalize them. Their conclusions will be colored by their own judgments and thinking. You must give them space to process in their own way.

Yur children's personal identities, interests, and preferences may diverge from paths you envisioned for them. You cannot bend their futures to your expectations; their autonomy must be respected.

We live in an increasingly diverse, connected world. Although we may long for the cultural homogeneity of earlier eras, globalization cannot be undone. Adapting to societal changes is necessary.

Time moves in one direction. The past is fixed, for better or worse. Lingering regret over "what might have been" or guilt about past mistakes distracts us from present growth.

The political climate reflects millions of variables. While positive change is possible, we alone cannot reshape the entire partisan landscape or undo entrenched polarization.

In matters of conscience and identity, forced conformity often breeds resentment. Our children's beliefs must be arrived at voluntarily, through their own exploration.

Though we cannot change others or society at large, we can change ourselves. By focusing inward, we gain the wisdom and empathy to build bridges with loved ones across divides. Our example can inspire.

Accepting these limits liberates us from frustration and paves the way for positive action. With an open and curious mindset, we engage others as they are - different, but no less worthy of our unconditional love.

Embracing Change and Adaptability

NAVIGATING RELATIONSHIPS with loved ones who have different political or social views can be challenging, especially for conservative parents and their non-conservative children. However, evolving as individuals and improving relationships isn't about abandoning core beliefs; it's about fostering growth, understanding, and adaptability.

Opening up to change shows a genuine commitment to understanding your children's experiences and perspectives. It creates an environment for dialogue, empathy, and mutual respect. Resistance to change often originates from fear—a fear of losing deeply held values or a sense of identity. Yet, embracing change is more about expanding one's understanding of the world and less about betraying core values.

Benefits abound when you decide to expand your horizons. You not only enrich your own life but also deepen your relationship with your children. The key is to actively seek out and engage in conversations that expose you to diverse viewpoints. Challenging your assumptions can broaden your understanding and help bridge any existing gaps in belief.

Recognizing the need for personal growth is essential. It prompts self-reflection, encouraging you to examine your beliefs and approach dialogues with curiosity and openness.

Such growth enhances not only your relationships but also sets a positive example for your children about the importance of adaptability.

To facilitate this change, arm yourself with practical strategies. Consider reading material from different perspectives, attending workshops, or engaging in conversations that challenge your viewpoint. When encountering fear or discomfort in the face of change, recognize that growth often happens outside comfort zones. Seek support to navigate these emotional landscapes; friends, family, or professionals can offer safe spaces for processing and perspective.

Building empathy is crucial. Actively listen and seek to understand your children's experiences and perspectives. This fosters an environment for honest dialogue and deeper connection. Finding common ground—even amidst political differences—can go a long way in fostering understanding and connection. Shared interests or values can be a great starting point.

Remember, personal growth is an ongoing journey. It demands a consistent effort, a readiness for new experiences, and self-reflection. Support and guidance can be incredibly beneficial along the way. Whether it's friends, family, or professionals, their insights can offer valuable perspectives and emotional support.

Don't forget to celebrate small victories. It's easy to get disheartened, but recognizing and appreciating every effort can keep you motivated. Moving forward with intentionality requires an ongoing commitment to openness, regular self-reflection, and proactive relationship nurturing.

Approaching any disagreements with the genuine desire to understand can create an environment where both growth and change are possible.

Embracing change and adaptability is transformative for anyone—conservative parents or not—seeking more harmonious relationships with loved ones of differing views. The journey involves ongoing self-reflection, resilience, and a commitment to lifelong learning. By taking these steps, you can navigate challenges, celebrate progress, and cultivate stronger, more meaningful connections.

Committing to Lifelong Learning

LIFELONG LEARNING ISN'T just a buzzword or a trend; it's a commitment to personal growth and understanding. For those who identify as conservative parents, embracing lifelong learning is crucial, especially when your beliefs and values may diverge from those of your non-conservative children. The onus is on you to bridge that gap through continued education and self-improvement.

The first step on this transformative journey is to explore a variety of learning opportunities. Consider reading books that challenge your current worldview, attending workshops that introduce you to different perspectives, enrolling in online courses to deepen your understanding, and engaging in meaningful conversations with people whose beliefs differ from your own. Each of these activities not only broadens your intellectual horizons but also makes you better equipped to understand the complex world your children are navigating.

Resistance to new ideas is a hurdle you might face. Your preconceived ideologies can create a barrier to embracing a commitment to lifelong learning. Address this resistance directly and find ways to overcome it. Cultivate an environment of curiosity and open-mindedness; this will serve as a safe space where your children can freely express themselves.

Incorporating learning into your daily routine is not just practical but also transformative. Set aside dedicated time for reading, seek out information from a variety of sources, and engage in regular dialogues with your children who might hold different views. By making lifelong learning an integral part of your life, you also become a role model for your children, reinforcing the value of growth and open-mindedness.

One of the most impactful outcomes of lifelong learning is the ability to develop empathy. Gaining insight into your non-conservative children's viewpoints and experiences allows for deeper connections and mutual understanding. Empathy is often the missing link between divergent beliefs, and a commitment to learning equips you with the tools needed to bridge that emotional and intellectual gap.

As times change, so must your perspectives. The world isn't static; it's a dynamic entity that evolves daily. This doesn't necessitate abandoning your core values, but it does mean adjusting your mindset in light of new information and societal shifts.

Seeking external support can be invaluable on this lifelong learning path. Whether through experts, therapists, or like-minded individuals who have navigated similar challenges, external perspectives can offer additional insights and serve as a form of encouragement and support.

Remember, lifelong learning is a continual process that demands consistent effort and commitment. View this not just as a personal development tool but as a way to improve your relationship with your children who hold different beliefs. The impact you can have on your family's overall dynamic can be both positive and lasting.

Your commitment to learning sets a precedent for your children. By living out these values, you encourage them to adopt a mindset of growth and open-mindedness, affecting their lives in a myriad of ways. Your actions often resonate more powerfully than your words ever could.

Along the journey, don't forget to celebrate the progress you make. It's important to acknowledge both the big milestones and the small victories. Each step towards change and adaptability strengthens your relationships and contributes to a more harmonious family environment.

The commitment to lifelong learning is indispensable for anyone looking to bridge the ideological gap within their family. Through continuous education, empathy, adaptability, and a network of support, stronger and more meaningful connections can be forged. Remember, this isn't a one-and-done deal; it requires ongoing effort, self-reflection, and a genuine desire to understand and connect. Together, we can navigate the complexities of modern family dynamics and cultivate relationships built on love, acceptance, and mutual respect.

Chapter 8: Reconnecting and Moving Forward

Initiating Reconnection

Reconnecting with people who hold non-conservative viewpoints is crucial for fostering a more compassionate and understanding dynamic within families or social circles. This is an opportunity to bridge ideological divides, regain lost trust, and establish relationships built on open communication and mutual respect. By taking the first steps toward reconnection, you can create a safe environment for open dialogue, encouraging a sense of belonging and acceptance.

If you're looking to reconnect with individuals who have non-conservative viewpoints, it's important to examine your own biases and beliefs. You must be willing to confront how your own convictions may have contributed to any disconnect or tension. It's through introspection and self-reflection that you can fully understand your role in these strained relationships and open the door to personal and relational growth.

Repairing trust and building connections requires time and patience. If you're embarking on a journey toward reconnection, it's important to set realistic expectations. Understand that change won't happen overnight and that there may be setbacks. Approach this process with an open mind, willing to listen to and learn from the perspectives of those with whom you seek to reconnect. By doing so, you're paving the way for meaningful conversations and relationships.

Starting conversations with people who hold different political views requires a fine balance of openness and respect. It's vital to create a non-judgmental space where others can express their thoughts freely, without fear of rejection or ridicule. Employing active listening and empathy can go a long way in facilitating effective communication. A sincere desire to understand their viewpoints can serve as the cornerstone for a more harmonious relationship.

One practical way to reconnect with people who have differing ideologies is by identifying common interests or shared activities. This could involve hobbies, community events, or other experiences that both parties enjoy. These shared moments offer an opportunity to strengthen relationships outside of ideological conflicts, providing a context for positive interaction and unity.

As you work on reconnecting, it's crucial to respect the boundaries and individual autonomy of those you're trying to understand better. Be careful not to cross the line between sharing your views and imposing them. Creating an environment where people feel heard and respected as individuals is essential. By honoring their perspectives and personal boundaries, you're showing a commitment to understanding and embracing their unique identities.

If challenges arise during your attempts to reconnect, it may be helpful to seek professional guidance. Family therapy or counseling can offer tools and strategies to help navigate the complexities of strained relationships. Remember, asking for help is not a sign of weakness but rather a proactive step towards strengthening bonds and enhancing communication.

Throughout your journey toward reconnection, it's important to celebrate any progress, no matter how small. Each step you take is a small victory worth acknowledging. Stay committed and patient, understanding that rebuilding relationships is an ongoing process. By continuously fostering open communication and empathy, you can create more loving and harmonious relationships with those who hold different viewpoints.

Rebuilding Shared Experiences

IN THE JOURNEY TO HELP you reconnect with children who don't share your conservative beliefs, the power of rebuilding shared experiences can't be overstated. Such experiences create the potential for new memories and can bridge ideological gaps. To mend and strengthen relationships with your children, it's essential to actively engage in shared activities. This becomes the foundation for mutual understanding, empathy, and rebuilt trust.

Before you create new shared experiences, consider reflecting on past interactions with your children. Remember both the highs and the lows, the laughter and the tears. Acknowledging both the positive and negative aspects of your past shared experiences can provide valuable insights. This will allow you to move forward with a mindset focused on openness, humility, and strengthening the familial bond.

When considering how to rebuild shared experiences, look for common interests and hobbies. This might require stepping out of your comfort zone, especially if these activities don't naturally align with conservative values. For instance, hiking, cooking, or gardening could be points of mutual interest. Finding such common ground creates an atmosphere where enjoyment and understanding can flourish.

Planning and creating meaningful moments with your children is another important step. Intentional efforts, such as brainstorming activities and setting mutual goals, display a commitment to reconnecting. Whether it's a road trip exploring new places, family game nights, or volunteering together, infusing these activities with purpose can result in lasting memories and a deepened connection.

In the age of technology, you have the option to rebuild shared experiences digitally. Virtual activities, video calls, and online games offer opportunities for connection that transcend physical distance. Adapting to your children's communication platforms shows your willingness to understand and nurture your relationship with them.

Effective communication and active listening are essential when engaging in shared experiences. Create a safe environment where your children can express their thoughts without fear of judgment or rejection. This involves asking open-ended questions and displaying genuine curiosity and empathy, laying the groundwork for a healthier relationship.

Regular family rituals and traditions can anchor your efforts to rebuild shared experiences. These rituals, whether they are weekly family dinners or yearly holidays, should be inclusive of differing beliefs. They offer a sense of belonging and unity that transcends ideological boundaries.

Collaboration on mutual projects and goals is another avenue for strengthening bonds. Joint efforts, such as home renovations, starting a family business, or charity work, create camaraderie and mutual respect. Aligning your actions toward a shared purpose fosters teamwork and open dialogue.

Allowing space for individuality and personal growth is crucial. Support your children's dreams, aspirations, and self-expression, even if they don't align with your beliefs. This sends a powerful message of unconditional love and acceptance, further strengthening your bond.

Celebrating milestones and achievements together can amplify the impact of shared experiences. Acknowledge and value each other's successes, regardless of any ideological divides. Such celebrations serve as affirmations that provide a strong foundation for a loving, inclusive relationship.

The intentional process of rebuilding shared experiences with your children holds transformative potential. By engaging in reflection, exploration, and meaningful activities, you can bridge ideological divides and foster an environment of understanding, empathy, and unconditional love. It's a journey that demands openness and commitment, but the rewards are immeasurable.

Respecting Boundaries and Autonomy

RESPECT ISN'T JUST a cornerstone for conservative parents; it's the bedrock for any thriving parent-child relationship. Regardless of your political beliefs, genuine respect accepts your child's individuality and autonomy, setting the stage for open communication and shared growth.

When you understand that your child is a separate person with their own thoughts and emotions, you're recognizing their personal boundaries. This acknowledgment doesn't undermine your role as a parent but rather strengthens it by nurturing independence and self-identity.

Physical, emotional, and intellectual boundaries each require their own kind of respect. Active listening and empathy become crucial tools for understanding these multiple layers. By honoring your child's individual boundaries, you foster an environment that opens the door to meaningful conversations and mutual respect.

Consent is a pivotal concept, encompassing everything from sharing personal information to physical touch. When you respect your child's consent, you're not just validating their autonomy; you're also teaching them an invaluable life lesson about mutual respect in relationships.

Allow your children the freedom to make their choices and learn from their experiences. While your guidance is important, avoiding the imposition of your own beliefs encourages their independence and builds a relationship rooted in trust.

Clarity in what you expect from the relationship eliminates ambiguity and avoids unintentional boundary violations. It helps to

articulate these expectations while also allowing space for your child's own perspectives.

A safe and transparent environment encourages your children to share their thoughts without fear of judgment.

Effective communication is a two-way street that includes active listening and empathy from both parties.

Your child's need for privacy should be respected. Whether it's physical space or digital boundaries, respecting privacy communicates trust and encourages responsible decision-making.

Model the behavior you want to see. Consistently demonstrate respectful communication, own up to your mistakes, and set good examples. This enables your child to develop their own healthy boundaries.

Conflicts are inevitable, but resolution is key. Approach disagreements with empathy and an open mind, striving to resolve issues in a way that respects everyone's autonomy and boundaries.

Teaching your child to advocate for themselves empowers them to set their boundaries and make their own choices, equipping them with vital life skills.

Build trust by honoring your child's boundaries and showing consistent support for their autonomy. A strong relationship thrives on trust, formed through mutual understanding and respect.

Being flexible means adjusting to your child's evolving boundaries and autonomy. This willingness to adapt and grow demonstrates your commitment to a dynamic, respectful relationship.

Take time to examine your own attitudes and behaviors to identify areas for growth. A relationship thrives best when both parties are aware of their own boundaries and committed to improving them.

Maintaining a consistent approach and reinforcing your commitment to respect will go a long way in nurturing a healthy, long-lasting relationship. After all, respect is a continuous commitment, not just a one-off act.

Modeling Civil Discourse

IN AN INCREASINGLY polarized political climate, it can be challenging to maintain civil discourse, especially when disagreements arise within families. As conservative parents, we have an opportunity to lead by example - demonstrating positive communication habits that can inspire our non-conservative children. By exemplifying compassionate and thoughtful discourse, we can pass down these values to guide interactions in the next generation.

First and foremost, civil discourse requires respecting the dignity of every individual. We should listen attentively when our children express their political views and avoid attacking their character or motivations when we disagree. By modeling respectful listening, we teach the importance of granting dignity to all.

When political conversations become tense, we must refrain from inflammatory language and personal attacks. Emotionally-charged rhetoric divides, while a calm and thoughtful tone builds bridges. We can demonstrate how to articulate viewpoints with care, focusing on bringing people together.

It is natural to feel defensive when our political values are challenged. However, we must avoid reacting defensively or shutting down differing opinions. By staying open-minded and responsive, we show how dissenting voices should be engaged with empathy, not combatively dismissed.

Fact-checking information and relying on evidence-based arguments set a standard of intellectual responsibility. We should verify claims and admit when we've made a mistake or spoken out of anger. These actions underscore the merits of careful, truthful discourse.

Understanding multiple perspectives is key. We should discuss political issues from different valid viewpoints, articulating arguments opposing our own stance reasonably. This models fairness, nuance and avoidance of oversimplification when tackling complex topics.

There are times when avoiding political conversations altogether is best. We might change the subject when discourse is unproductive or emotions are running high. This shows that timing and setting are important considerations in sensitive discussions.

By exemplifying thoughtful, compassionate and intellectually honest discourse, conservative parents can make civil communication the norm, not the exception. Our example provides a powerful lesson in the value of bridging divides with wisdom and care - a legacy for future generations.

Maintaining Hope and Perspective

WHEN POLITICAL DIFFERENCES strain family relationships, it can be challenging to remain hopeful and maintain proper perspective. However, nurturing optimism and centering ourselves on what truly matters helps sustain us through periods of difficulty and discord. By cultivating resilience, we can continue striving to bridge divides with love.

First, we must keep in mind that a single conversation or disagreement does not define an entire relationship. One heated debate or moment of tension amid years of shared love and memories does not spell failure. Ups and downs are natural; our connections endure.

Though progress may seem incremental, small changes achieved through consistent effort compound. We must measure successes over the long term, not day-to-day. Celebrating minor breakthroughs sustains motivation to enact gradual transformation.

There is power in reaffirming our love and commitment, even if tangible results are lacking. The simple acts of showing affection and spending quality time together strengthen bonds, whether or not political views align. Shared joy matters more than unanimity.

When frustrated, it helps to seek inspiration from families who have overcome greater ideological rifts. Their success and wisdom can reenergize our own efforts. With empathy and care, no divide is insurmountable.

We must be wary of catastrophizing and making sweeping generalizations when tensions run high. Nuance provides balance; no single disagreement or bad day defines the entire relationship.

Above all, nurturing personal serenity helps maintain proper perspective. Through mindfulness, prayer or meditation, we center ourselves on the ideals of understanding and compassion. Clarity of purpose sustains us.

With psychological resilience and unwavering love, we persist through challenges. Guided by hope, even the deepest divides between loved ones can be bridged one day at a time. Faith and fortitude light the way.

Celebrating Differences and Diversity

CELEBRATING DIFFERENCES and diversity within the family is crucial for fostering positive family dynamics and relationships. It is an acknowledgment that each family member brings their own unique perspectives, experiences, and identities to the table. By embracing these differences, we create a more accepting and inclusive environment that values and celebrates the individuality of each family member. Rather than viewing diversity as a problem, we recognize it as a strength that enriches our family life.

Each family member possesses their own individuality and uniqueness, and by recognizing and valuing these qualities, we contribute to a more accepting and inclusive family environment. Embracing these differences means accepting that each person has their own thoughts, beliefs, and opinions, even if they differ from our own. It involves appreciating the diversity of perspectives and experiences within our family unit, understanding that these differences contribute to a more well-rounded and vibrant family dynamic.

Open and respectful communication is essential when discussing differences and diversity within the family. It is crucial to create a space where family members feel comfortable expressing their thoughts, feelings, and experiences, even when they differ from one another. By promoting healthy discussions, avoiding conflict, and actively listening to one another, we foster an environment that values and encourages diverse perspectives. It is important to approach these conversations with empathy, seeking to understand rather than to persuade or judge.

As parents, it is your role to teach acceptance and empathy towards different perspectives and experiences. This means fostering an understanding that differences should not be seen as obstacles, but as opportunities for growth and learning. You can cultivate these qualities within the family by encouraging our children to step outside their comfort zones, engage in activities that expose them to diverse perspectives and cultures, and by practicing empathy in our everyday interactions. By doing so, you develop a family that is compassionate, inclusive, and accepting.

Expanding cultural awareness and knowledge is an essential aspect of celebrating differences and diversity within the family. It involves actively seeking to learn about different cultures, traditions, and perspectives. We can do this by reading books, watching documentaries, attending cultural events, and engaging in conversations with individuals from diverse backgrounds. By expanding our cultural awareness, we develop a deeper respect and appreciation for the diversity that exists in our world.

In order to truly celebrate differences and diversity, it is important to incorporate diverse traditions and celebrations into our family gatherings. This means recognizing and valuing the traditions of all family members, regardless of their differences. By actively involving everyone in the planning and execution of family traditions and celebrations, we create a sense of inclusivity and belonging for all family members. This also provides an opportunity for learning and understanding different cultural practices and customs.

Creating a safe space where family members can authentically express themselves without fear of judgment or ridicule is crucial for celebrating differences and diversity. This means fostering an environment that encourages open-mindedness, actively listening, and non-judgmental responses. By creating a safe space, we show that everyone's voice is valued and respected, regardless of their differences. This allows each family member to feel comfortable sharing their thoughts, feelings, and experiences, facilitating deeper connections and understanding.

In order to embrace and celebrate differences, it is important to encourage collaboration and cooperation within the family. By working together towards shared goals and objectives, we bridge divides and strengthen family bonds. This involves recognizing the valuable contributions that each family member can bring to the table, regardless of their differences. By encouraging collaboration and cooperation, we create a sense of unity and togetherness that transcends individual differences.

An integral part of celebrating differences and diversity is recognizing and celebrating the achievements and contributions of all family members, regardless of their differences. By showcasing appreciation and support for each individual's unique talents and strengths, we create an environment that values and celebrates diversity. This builds self-esteem, fosters a sense of belonging, and reinforces the notion that every family member is valued and important.

As parents, it is your responsibility to instill values of equality and inclusivity within the family. This means treating each family member with respect and fairness, regardless of their differences. It involves encouraging open-mindedness and challenging discriminatory attitudes or behaviors. By incorporating these values into daily family life and decision-making processes, you create a foundation for a family that is built on equality and inclusivity.

While celebrating differences and diversity begins within the family, it is important to extend this mindset beyond the family setting. Teaching our children to value and embrace differences in the world involves exposing them to diverse cultures, perspectives, and experiences. This can be done through travel, community involvement, and seeking out opportunities to engage with individuals from different backgrounds. By doing so, we raise children who are compassionate, understanding, and respectful towards all people.

Ultimately, celebrating differences and diversity should be viewed as a lasting legacy that we pass down through generations. By valuing and embracing diversity within our own family, we leave a lasting impact on future family relationships and dynamics. This legacy extends beyond our immediate family and influences how our children will raise their own families, fostering a society that values and celebrates differences. As conservatives, embracing diversity within our families allows us to create a more inclusive and united society that appreciates the richness of our differences.

Embracing Unconditional Love

IN THE MIDST OF POLITICAL differences and strained relationships with our non-conservative children, it can be easy to lose sight of the power of unconditional love. Yet, it is precisely this love that holds the key to healing and growth in our parent-child relationships. Unconditional love is a love that surpasses politics and ideologies, transcending our differences and allowing us to see the humanity in one another. It is a love that says, "I may not agree with your beliefs, but I love you unconditionally nonetheless."

Embracing unconditional love as a conservative parent is not without its challenges. Our deeply held beliefs and values can make it difficult for us to embrace ideas and perspectives that contradict our own. We may feel compelled to hold firm to our convictions and may struggle to understand how to love someone whose beliefs differ so greatly from our own. But it is precisely in these moments of challenge that unconditional love has the potential to make the greatest impact.

When we choose to embrace unconditional love, we open the door to a deeper understanding, empathy, and connection with our non-conservative children. We begin to see them as individuals with their own unique experiences, rather than simply as political adversaries. Through our love and acceptance, we create an environment where honest conversations can take place, where genuine understanding can be cultivated, and where bridges can be built.

The power of unconditional love can be seen in countless examples and anecdotes of transformed parent-child relationships. Stories of conservative parents who have embraced unconditional love and acceptance, despite their differing beliefs, serve as powerful reminders of the potential for change and growth. These stories remind us that it is never too late to bridge the gap and create a bond built on love and understanding.

Forgiveness is an integral part of embracing unconditional love. When we forgive, we let go of resentment and bitterness that may have built up over time. We recognize that we are all imperfect beings who make mistakes and hold differing opinions. Forgiveness allows us to heal the wounds that have divided us and paves the way for reconciliation and healing. It allows us to move forward with a renewed sense of compassion and acceptance.

Acceptance is another crucial aspect of embracing unconditional love. It means acknowledging and respecting our differences, while also finding common ground. Acceptance is not about changing or compromising our beliefs, but rather about finding ways to coexist and appreciate one another despite those differences. It is about embracing the idea that love can transcend political boundaries and that our relationships are worth nurturing, even if we may never fully agree on every issue.

Cultivating unconditional love in the parent-child relationship requires effort, patience, and a commitment to personal growth. It means actively listening to our children, seeking to understand their perspectives, and engaging in open and honest communication. It also means setting healthy boundaries, respecting one another's autonomy, and not allowing our differences to define our relationship. It requires a willingness to self-reflect, to challenge our own biases, and to continually strive for growth and understanding.

The benefits of embracing unconditional love are immeasurable. It leads to increased happiness, fulfillment, and a stronger bond with our non-conservative children. It allows us to be present in their lives, to support them, and to celebrate their successes, regardless of our political differences. It helps us create a home environment that is rooted in love, acceptance, and respect, and serves as a powerful example to future generations.

To you conservative parents who may be feeling overwhelmed or discouraged in their journey towards embracing unconditional love, I want to offer my support and encouragement. This is not an easy path, but it is a worthwhile one. It is a journey that requires us to continually work on ourselves, to challenge our own biases, and to extend grace and understanding to those who may see the world differently. It is a journey that requires patience, forgiveness, and a commitment to growth. But it is a journey that holds the potential for tremendous healing, growth, and transformation.

Embracing unconditional love is not a one-time act, but an ongoing commitment. It requires consistent effort, understanding, and a willingness to evolve alongside our non-conservative children. It is a journey that will have its ups and downs, but the rewards are immeasurable.

Finally, I want to emphasize the importance of community and support networks in the process of embracing unconditional love. Surrounding ourselves with like-minded individuals who can provide guidance, understanding, and encouragement can make all the difference. Whether it be through support groups, online communities, or trusted friends, finding a community of individuals who share our values and can offer support on this journey is invaluable.

Embracing unconditional love is a powerful way for conservative parents to bridge the gap with our non-conservative children. It requires us to challenge our beliefs, be open to growth, and release the need for control. By choosing to love unconditionally, we create a space for healing, understanding, and connection. We not only transform our parent-child relationships but also contribute to a wider societal and political landscape that is more compassionate, inclusive, and accepting. Let us embark on this journey together and create a world where love knows no boundaries.

Chapter 9: Closing Remarks

Empathy Is The Key

Empathy is the golden thread woven throughout this entire book, and for good reason. Empathy serves as the very foundation for bridging ideological divides, healing strained relationships, and fostering understanding between those we perceive as different from ourselves – including our own children.

In the context of the complex dynamics between conservative parents and their increasingly non-conservative adult children, empathy takes on a profoundly important role. By continually striving to understand our children's evolving perspectives, life experiences, and emotions, the act of cultivating empathy becomes transformative. It holds the power to shift mindsets, challenge assumptions, and open new pathways of connection.

But what exactly is empathy? And why does it matter so much when it comes to bridging generational and political divides within our families?

Empathy Defined

In simple terms, empathy is the ability to understand and share the feelings and experiences of another person. It goes beyond sympathy, which is feeling sorrow or concern for someone's suffering. Empathy takes it a step further – it involves emotionally connecting with others by imagining what it would be like to be in their situation.

The essence of empathy is being able to step outside of your own reality and perspective, and to immerse yourself in the emotions, perceptions, and motivations of another. It enables you to see the world through their eyes.

True empathy requires more than just imagining or approximating what someone else feels. We have to suspend our biases, judgments, and preconceived notions in order to fully understand their inner experiences. It demands that we tune into the context, stories, and vulnerabilities that shape their worldview. Only then can we gain true insight into their emotions.

Why Conservative Parents Must Prioritize Empathy

Developing empathy is crucial for conservative parents seeking to reconnect with their non-conservative adult children. Without empathy, communication breaks down, relationships fracture, and the ideological divide widens.

For conservative parents, stepping into the shoes of their non-conservative children may feel challenging at first. Your life experiences, values, and political outlook differ greatly from those of your children. You may struggle to relate to or understand perspectives so divergent from your own.

However, empathy holds the key to overcoming these hurdles. By tapping into the power of empathy, you can gain deeper insight into the forces and influences that shaped your children's beliefs and values. With empathy, you can better appreciate why they care so passionately about causes that may seem incomprehensible to you. You can understand how societal changes and generational dynamics informed their worldviews.

Most importantly, empathy allows you to see your children not merely as opponents on the other side of a political divide, but as complex human beings navigating an increasingly complex world. With empathy, they become more than just stereotyped caricatures - they become real people, with real experiences that matter.

The act of stepping into their shoes through empathy does not mean you must agree with their stances or compromise your own values. But choosing to genuinely understand their perspective represents an opportunity to strengthen the bond that goes beyond politics – the sacred parent-child relationship.

Why Empathy Matters More Than Ever

America's current political and social climate is more polarized than ever before. This polarization inevitably seeps into family dynamics, souring relationships and threatening communication between loved ones.

For conservative parents and their Gen Z or millennial children living in this divisive era, empathy serves as a crucial tool for rising above the partisan fray and reconnecting on a human level.

Unlike previous generations, today's youth are digital natives who grew up in an interconnected online landscape that exposed them to perspectives vastly different from preceding generations'. Their social circles are diverse; their news feeds expansive and crowded. The pace of change accelerated rapidly, informing their values and priorities in new ways.

To conservative parents anchored in more traditional values, the outlook of their children can seem utterly foreign at times. Their calls for sweeping social reform and notions of identity and social justice may appear to undermine conservatism's core tenets of limited government and personal responsibility.

These fundamental disconnects in how younger Americans perceive the world have driven the rise of movements like Black Lives Matter, debates around gender identity, and causes like climate action. Their perspectives reflect lived experiences and values shaped by events such as 9/11, the Great Recession, Covid-19, and other seismic cultural shifts.

For generations coming of age amidst such turbulence, notions of order, continuity, and "traditional values" carry little weight. As conservative parents, we may yearn for the America we knew growing up. But we must also seek to understand the forces that shaped our children's diverging outlooks.

This is precisely why empathy is needed now more than ever before. America feels almost like two separate nations inhabiting one land, divided by cavernous gaps of misunderstanding. Our children's perspectives and motivations often feel alien. But it is possible to cross that chasm through humble empathy.

How to Develop Empathy

Empathy is a skill that can be nurtured through practice. By consistently engaging in small acts of attempting to understand others, we strengthen our "empathy muscles", making it easier over time. Here are some practical steps conservative parents can take to enhance empathy:

WHY WON'T MY CHILDREN TALK TO ME? A BOOK FOR CONSERVATIVES

Listen without judgment: Give your full attention when your child expresses thoughts or emotions. Don't interrupt or immediately voice disagreement. Just focus on understanding.

Ask thoughtful questions: Inquire about how events, experiences, or challenges impacted your child's perspectives and emotions. Seek to learn about factors you may have overlooked.

Suspend assumptions: We often project motivations or make assumptions about others' beliefs that are inaccurate. Catch yourself when making assumptions about your child's stances.

Reflect on your biases: We all harbor implicit biases. Slow down and notice when one affects your ability to empathize with your child's viewpoint. Strive to overcome it.

Express understanding: Let your child know you appreciate the emotions and reasoning behind their perspective, even if you don't fully agree. Validation builds trust and connection.

Immerse in their experiences: Engage in activities together that offer insight into causes or communities your child cares about. Experiencing, not just discussing, builds empathy.

Read widely: Expand your knowledge of social issues and generational change so you can better understand the cultural influences that shaped your child's mindset.

Practice mindfulness: Meditation and mindfulness exercises strengthen self-awareness and emotional intelligence, which enhances our ability to empathize.

Seek common ground: Focus on finding shared values and aspirations rather than just political disagreements. Mutual hopes and goals unite.

Be patient and persistent: Empathy is a muscle. It requires regular exercise through consistent practice and small daily acts of understanding. Change takes time.

Reap the Rewards

While empathy can feel challenging at first, embracing it brings immense rewards that make the effort more than worthwhile.

By striving to empathize with your non-conservative children, you open the door to honest and thoughtful conversations about complex issues. With empathy, they know you see them as a full person, not just an opponent. This builds trust and a willingness to be vulnerable.

You gain insight into factors influencing them that you missed before, like experiences with discrimination, economic instability, or mental health challenges. Your relationship deepens as you better appreciate their inner world.

Moments of connection and joy become more frequent, from shared laughs over childhood memories to partaking in new activities together. Empathy dissolves the perception of separation.

Your example of choosing understanding inspires them and becomes a positive influence. They learn the power of empathy to create change, modeling it in their own relationships and breaking cycles of discord.

With empathy, your child sees your relationship is valued beyond politics. The lifelong bond between parent and child, though tested, will emerge stronger. Hope for reconnection endures.

By walking in another's shoes, we expand our horizons while staying grounded in love. In this fractious world, empathy remains a revolutionary force - the key to unlocking our shared humanity.

Looking Inward

AS CONSERVATIVE PARENTS, fostering greater empathy and connection with your non-conservative children necessitates a willingness to courageously look inward.

Self-reflection requires asking difficult questions, challenging long-held assumptions, and confronting our own limitations and biases with radical honesty. This introspective journey can feel uncomfortable at times. However, embracing the discomfort is necessary for growth.

When we commit to looking inward, we peel back the layers shrouding our perspectives. We gain clearer insight into the forces and experiences that shaped our beliefs over decades. The blind spots, inconsistencies, and areas of resistance become visible.

This understanding empowers us to adapt and expand our mindsets. We shed the rigidity that strained our relationships and prevented us from truly appreciating our child's worldview.

The path of self-reflection contains twists and turns. At times, we may stumble or hit roadblocks. Frustration and uncertainty will arise. However, by persistently focusing our energy inward on self-growth, rather than attempting to change others, we plant seeds for positive change in our relationships.

Why Self-Reflection Matters

Engaging in honest self-reflection may seem unnecessary or even counterproductive for some conservative parents. We may feel our beliefs are time-tested and unshakeable. Or that marriage, raising children, and professional success prove the soundness of our principles.

However, the disconnection from our own adult children indicates that certain long-unchallenged assumptions require re-examination. Their differing life experiences reveal gaps in our understanding of this rapidly changing world.

Your children's beliefs reflect realities and hardships that your generation did not face in the same way. As the planet warms, inequality grows, and cultural diversity expands, our children navigate a volatile world.

Self-reflection enables us to confront how our own upbringing and values systems may not fully equip us to understand the perspectives of those coming of age under vastly different circumstances. We recognize where resistance to societal change still lingers within us, limiting our capacity for empathy.

This journey is not about abandoning core principles. Our beliefs hold wisdom and value worth preserving. However, by identifying blind spots and areas of bias, we can broaden our thinking. This strengthens relationships with our children and allows conservatism to evolve for new eras.

HOW TO REFLECT

Embracing rigorous self-examination is challenging. Where do we start? What questions should we ask? Here are some practices that can guide the process:

● Observe your automatic reactions when discussing sensitive issues with your child. Do certain comments elicit feelings of anger or defensiveness? Ask yourself where these reactions originate.

● Reflect on your upbringing. How did your parents' beliefs and values shape your worldview? Did certain messages restrict your perspectives or create unquestioned assumptions?

● Consider how changing historical and cultural contexts impacted your outlook. For example, how did events like the Cold War or the political climate of your youth inform your beliefs differently than your child's generation?

● Identify any hypocrisies or inconsistencies in your stances. For example, do you advocate for small government except for policies that align with your moral values?

● Notice when your opinion is rooted more in emotion than facts. For example, does fear or disgust toward groups like immigrants drive your political stances more than data?

● Question the assumptions you hold about groups different from yourself. Ask yourself if these beliefs stem from direct experiences and facts or stereotypes and generalizations.

● Examine your news diet. Does it provide balanced coverage explaining multiple valid perspectives? Or does it primarily reinforce pre-existing biases?

● Explore your motivations when political conversations become heated. Do you prioritize "winning" arguments over mutual understanding?

● Consider how privilege may have blinded you to the challenges others face. For example, systemic racism or sexual orientation discrimination.

● Reflect on what values you prioritize when making political decisions. For example, does loyalty or tradition outweigh a commitment to equality for you?

Of course, self-reflection should not be limited to this starter list. It is an ongoing process of questioning assumptions, identifying blind spots, and recognizing areas for growth. Over time, these practices can reveal limited mindsets while strengthening discernment.

Gain Clarity from Within

Peeling back internal layers often reveals contradictions between our stated principles and actual behaviors. For example, we may profess a belief that all humans deserve equal dignity. But subconscious prejudice toward certain groups can persist.

By identifying these discrepancies through self-reflection, we gain the clarity needed to realign our external actions with internal values. Our behavior then becomes more consistent with our convictions. We embody our principles.

This clarity provides a moral anchor amidst the complexity of modern society. Rather than reacting from fear or anger when facing change, we respond from a place of purpose. Our inner compass guides us.

Reflect on Relationships

An honest inventory of past interactions with our children can reveal patterns that limited mutual understanding. Observing these tendencies with detachment allows them to be addressed.

For example, the impulse to lecture rather than listen often hinders productive dialogue. Or reflexively invalidating emotions shuts down vulnerability. An over-emphasis on problem-solving rather than just empathizing can also strain communication.

By becoming aware of these dynamics through self-reflection, we can consciously cultivate more constructive habits. We shift from reactive to responsive, creating an atmosphere that fosters mutual understanding and respect.

Discover Common Ground

Despite surface-level differences, exploration often reveals shared values and aspirations between parents and children. We hold these timeless ideals in common: human dignity, justice, community, knowledge, beauty, family.

By looking inward, we remember this common ground. Political tactics and rhetoric can obscure what unites us. But reflecting on fundamental shared hopes cuts through the noise.

We gain renewed appreciation for the principles we hold in common with loved ones across generations. This empowers us to have faith in one another's essential goodness. Understanding blossoms.

Growth Begins Within

Self-reflection is not a finite endeavor, but a lifelong process. Our children's growth never ceases; neither must our own. By regularly looking inward, we nurture the empathy, discernment and clarity needed to meet this moment.

Of course, this journey will have ups and downs. Not every moment of self-reflection will be perfectly smooth or comfortable. There may be setbacks and resistance.

However, by embracing this inner work, we take responsibility for our own evolution. Rather than focusing on changing others, positive transformation begins from within. We must be the change we seek.

As we courageously explore our inner landscape, we gain self-knowledge and adaptability. We shed rigidity and embrace growth, creating space for open-mindedness.

This strengthens our ability to build bridges, empowering us to forge connections grounded in understanding and renewed trust. We embody grace and wisdom.

The light of awareness illuminates all that we are – both strengths and shadows alike. By looking inward, we harness our full potential for empathy and growth.

The greatest seeds of change are planted within. Watered by reflection and care, our inner landscapes bloom into bridges to understanding and fulfillment.

Moving Forward in Hope

WITH EMPATHY AND SELF-understanding as our guides, we move forward with hope. We accept that while some political differences may remain with our children, our shared humanity runs far deeper than any partisan divide.

This is not the end, but rather the beginning of an exciting new chapter in our relationship. The journey here was not always smooth. There were heartaches and setbacks. Moments when the distance between us felt unbridgeable.

However, by taking the first steps - listening, learning, reflecting, understanding - we have built bridges where once there were only walls. Our connections have been reaffirmed and strengthened. Common ground has emerged through the fog.

Though the ideological gap between generations persists, the relational gap between us as parents and children has narrowed. Where silence once prevailed, now communication flows more freely. Where trust had eroded, foundations have been repaired. Where our differences were once condemned, now diversity is celebrated.

What fuels this sense of hope for the future, despite remaining political differences? By walking this path together, we have come to see that our love and shared humanity transcend the binaries of left versus right. While external forces seek to divide us, our bonds prove that unity is possible.

Nurturing Understanding

This hope-filled vision of the future is not naive or idealistic. We are under no illusions that overcoming polarization will be quick or easy. Challenges inevitably await us.

However, we now face these trials armed with the power of understanding. Our horizons have expanded through exercising empathy. We have gained priceless insight into what motivates our children's passions and concerns.

Rather than reacting out of confusion or fear towards their advocacy for social causes, we have built knowledge of the experiences shaping their worldview. By learning their stories, we gained appreciation for their resilience and vision.

This understanding cultivated through empathy does not mean blind acceptance. As parents, we still worry at times about certain choices or risky behaviors. We do not have to validate every idea to validate the person.

But this understanding has opened up new vistas for cooperation. We identify shared hopes that transcend divisions: justice, community, freedom, truth. By anchoring to these common values, we can move forward side-by-side.

Reconciling Differences

Achieving mutual understanding does not equal absolute agreement. Your core convictions will still clash with your child's at times. This leads to arguments, anxiety, sleepless nights.

But with empathy and open communication as your tools, these conflicts need not rupture relationships. You can learn to reconcile differences with maturity, wisdom and trust that your bond will endure.

First, grant each other good faith in disagreements. Assume your child holds their position due to actual experiences or careful reflection, not just youthful rebellion. Offer them the same benefit of the doubt you would want.

Next, try to identify the values at the root of a stance, not just its outward manifestation. For example, recognize that supporting gun restrictions stems from valuing human life. This builds a basis for respectful dialogue.

Also, distinguish between opinions about policy and judgments of character. You can ardently disagree with choices while still appreciating your child's humanity. Separate principles from personal attacks.

Focus on articulating your own positions positively rather than negatively characterizing your child's views. Don't define yourself by what you oppose, but what you support. What vision aligns with your values?

Look for resolution, not retribution. Conversations should strengthen understanding, not stroke egos. Be willing to agree to disagree and still affirm mutual respect and care.

With time and experience, you can become more adept at reconciling differences without severing ties. Patience, courage and faith in your shared principles make this possible.

A Legacy of Love

This journey has always been about more than just you and your child. It is a legacy you pass down to future generations. Your actions today set the tone for families tomorrow.

By choosing understanding over polarization, empathy over demonization, you counter society's dangerous trends. Your unconditional love defies labels. You set an example of possibility - that relationships can be nurtured across the deepest divides.

In the decades ahead, political tribalism may still exert its pull. But your family will have a counternarrative: conservatives and progressives dwelling in harmony because they chose understanding. A microcosm of unity that exposes polarization's emptiness.

Imagine your grandchildren gathering for holidays, conversing with ease. They inherited the tools to reconcile respectfully. Laughter, not shouting, fills the room. The seeds you planted bore bountiful fruit.

Of course, each new generation must learn for themselves how to cultivate understanding amidst difference. Your family won't be immune from future bumps in the road. But the foundation of mutual trust and respect you laid increases the odds of weathering whatever may come.

By walking this path, you ensured your family will see politics as secondary to the love that binds you. They grew up witnessing reconciliation firsthand. Now they are empowered to serve as ambassadors of empathy in an increasingly fractured world.

The Cycle is Broken

Society follows familiar cycles: generations clash, divisions deepen, frustrated efforts are made to bridge gaps. It is the perpetual rising and falling of tides.

But something powerful happens when enough families turn the tide - when parents and children come together as yours have. Like the famous "hundredth monkey effect", their reconciliation flames the spark of transformation.

It signals to a weary, cynical society that another way exists. Where demonization runs rampant, they show how listening and learning can heal. They offer living proof that walls between loved ones can indeed be dismantled - one self-reflection, honest conversation and act of empathy at a time.

This truth, once unleashed, takes on momentum of its own. It ignites imagination and hope in the disillusioned. It empowers others to follow their example in bridging divides close to home. Slowly but surely, the cascading impact is felt.

Of course, you will likely never see the full fruits of your sacrifice and courage. But have faith that your reconciliation nourishes this hunger for human connection. It cascades through networks known and unseen. Your light kindles more light.

In this profound sense, you become true pioneers and pathmakers. By courageously seeking understanding with your child, you point society towards a brighter future.

This cycle of parents and children growing apart, which once felt inevitable, is revealed as a tragic illusion. Its perceived permanence found false. Its grip, loosened.

In its place, a new reality emerges. Where open hearts and inquisitive minds pave the way to human flourishing. Where shared principles prove more powerful than divisions. Where grace and understanding reign.

The Journey is Just Beginning

Parents often speak of sacred duties owed to children. But children also awaken our highest selves. Their curiosity, idealism and willingness to question remind us not to sink complacently into old ways.

Through this experience with your child, you have been given a precious gift - the opportunity to become the best version of yourself. You exercised muscles of empathy and courage that may have atrophied over the years. Together, you have grown.

Of course, a single breakthrough conversation will not erase a lifetime of diverging experiences. Time and effort are required to sustain this renewed mutual understanding and implement lasting change.

There will be moments of frustration and miscommunication still. Feelings may still be hurt at times. The ideological gap may persist. But you are no longer estranged on opposite sides of a chasm.

Future challenges are not to be feared, but embraced. Each is an opportunity to practice forgiveness, deepen trust, and reaffirm the love that binds you beyond beliefs. You do this together, side by side.

In this sense, peaceful resolution is not a naively utopian dream. It is a daily practice, founded on empathy, wisdom and faith in our shared bonds. It is a garden to be continuously tended.

Your child set out on the open-ended journey of life. You, as parent, forged a different path - one leading to your own inward renewal. By taking this road less traveled, you broke free from ways of relating that no longer serve.

What matters most has come into clearer focus. Not winning arguments, but connecting with loved ones. Not political score-keeping, but cherishing each moment you are given. Not blind loyalty to party, but exercising discernment guided by conscience.

There will be missteps ahead and essential lessons still awaiting you both. But you do not walk this road alone. Your family is united by understanding and acceptance.

Together, you move forward in hope.

Don't miss out!

Visit the website below and you can sign up to receive emails whenever Bradley Hall publishes a new book. There's no charge and no obligation.

https://books2read.com/r/B-A-SCSZ-GDVNC

BOOKS2READ

Connecting independent readers to independent writers.

Did you love *Why Won't My Children Talk to Me? A Book For Conservatives*? Then you should read *The Enneagram and Money*[1] by Bradley Hall!

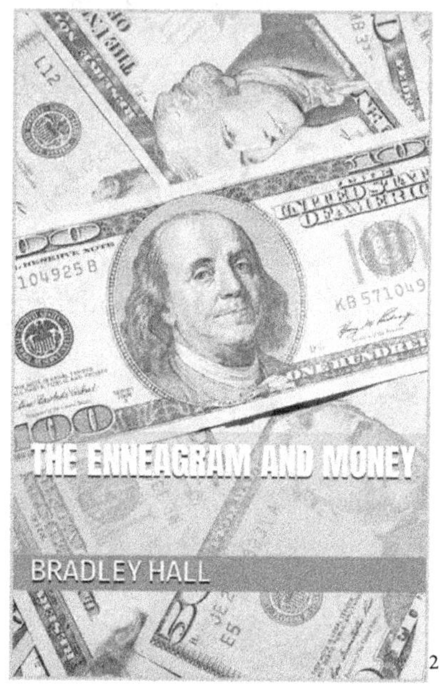

[2]

Unlock the secrets to financial empowerment with this in-depth exploration of the Enneagram and money. This groundbreaking book delves into the core motivations, fears, and unconscious patterns of each Enneagram type and how they influence financial behaviors. Discover how your personality shapes your relationship with money and gain profound insights to transform limiting financial patterns.

---

1. https://books2read.com/u/3GGpJr

2. https://books2read.com/u/3GGpJr

Through fascinating explorations of each type, from the Perfectionist to the Peacemaker, this book provides a roadmap to align your values, passions, and actions with your financial life. Overcome self-sabotaging behaviors, cultivate abundance and gratitude, and make conscious money choices that pave the way to genuine fulfillment and prosperity.

Within these pages, finance expert Bradley Hall blends their expertise in Enneagram personality types and financial dynamics to offer practical tips and exercises tailored to your unique needs. This allows you to leverage your natural strengths, overcome weaknesses, and establish financial balance and well-being.

Whether you're an Enneagram enthusiast or simply seeking financial wisdom, this book provides invaluable tools to master your money mindset. By embracing your core motivations and integrating your personality with your financial goals, you can embark on a transformative journey to financial authenticity and abundance.

Also by Bradley Hall

The Enneagram and Money
Why Won't My Children Talk to Me? A Book For
Conservatives

About the Author

Bradley Hall is a personal finance and tax expert living in Raleigh, NC with his wife, Amanda, and their dog, Yelena.

Originally from Jacksonville, FL, Bradley has attended the University of North Florida where he was conferred with a BA degree in Psychology, and Western Carolina University where he received his BA in Finance.

He writes about topics that interest him.

www.ingramcontent.com/pod-product-compliance
Lightning Source LLC
Chambersburg PA
CBHW070515160726
48003CB00004B/1576